Quilted
Landscapes

Machine-Embellished Fabric Images

Joan Blalock

That Patchwork Place®

Acknowledgments

A special thank you to those friends who became my students and made quilts for the Gallery. Many of you have surpassed the teacher. This is a much nicer book because of your efforts.

So many have helped to make this book possible. My deepest thanks to all of you.

First, to my husband Blay, for not complaining as my obsession with quilting expanded and took over his space (and sometimes his dinner). Thanks for your support.

To Joey and Mark Jr., my live-in grandsons who have learned to design their own quilts while Gram is working—thereby, making it possible for me to continue working on my projects.

To all the members of my quilt guild, The Southern Comforters of Bowie. I have learned so much from and been inspired by all of you.

To Holice Turnbow, who lectured to us in 1994. I doubt if he had any idea he'd start this project when he said, "If you have a good idea or a new method, write it!"

To the staff at That Patchwork Place for its willingness to consider a manuscript from an unknown quilter, especially to Ursula Reikes for her encouragement and Laura M. Reinstatler for her gentle way of keeping this writer "linear" when my inclination was to ramble. Thanks to Brian Metz for the beautiful artwork and to Amy Shayne for the text design—especially the wonderful cover.

Dedication

This book is dedicated to my mom, Evelyn Hoelscher Whitcomb, who patiently taught me to sew despite my penchant for ignoring the rules, for always being my friend, and for finding the tornado. I love you, Mom

Credits

Managing Editor	Greg Sharp
Technical Editor	Laura M. Reinstatler
Copy Editor	Liz McGehee
Proofreader	Melissa Riesland
Illustrator	Brian Metz
Photographer	Brent Kane
Design Director	Judy Petry
Text and Cover Designer	Amy Shayne
Production Assistants	Shean Bemis
	Dani Ritchardson

MISSION STATEMENT

WE ARE DEDICATED TO PROVIDING QUALITY PRODUCTS AND SERVICES THAT INSPIRE CREATIVITY. WE WORK TOGETHER TO ENRICH THE LIVES WE TOUCH.

That Patchwork Place is a financially responsible ESOP company.

Printed in the United States of America
01 00 99 98   6 5

Library of Congress Cataloging-in-Publication Data
Blalock, Joan
 Quilted landscapes : machine-embellished fabric images / by Joan Blalock.
  p. cm.
 Includes bibliographical references.
 ISBN 1-56477-144-X
 1. Patchwork—Patterns. 2. Machine quilting.
 3. Landscapes in art. I. Title
 TT835.B5117 1996
 746.46'0433—dc20   95-48414
                               CIP

Quilted Landscapes:
Machine-Embellished Fabric Images
© 1996 by Joan Blalock
That Patchwork Place, Inc., PO Box 118
Bothell, WA 98041-0118 USA

Table of Contents

Introduction ——————— 4

Designing the Quilt ——— 5

Supplies and Materials ——— 6
  Fabrics ————————— 6
  Color ——————————— 7
  Fabric Preparation ———— 9
  Sewing Machine ————— 10
  Thread ————————— 10
  Paper, Pencils, and Carbon Paper 10
  Paints, Inks, and Markers ——— 11
  Miscellaneous Supplies ——— 11

Basic Method ——————— 12
  Sunset ————————— 12
  Making the Master Pattern —— 13
  Making the Construction Pattern 15
  Assembly ————————— 16
    String Piecing ——————— 16
    Joining Sections ——————— 19
    Preparing to Quilt ————— 21
    Quilting ————————— 22
  Adding the Borders ———— 23
    Skewed Log Cabin Borders —— 23
    Mitered Borders ————— 24
  Adding the Binding ———— 26
  Making a Hanging Sleeve ——— 27

Gallery ——————————— 28

Embellishing the Landscape – 42
  General Information ————— 42
  Supplies for Embellishments —— 43

Projects ——————————— 44
  Cabin in the Pines ————— 44
  Sunset II ————————— 48
  At the Beach ——————— 52
  Fall Tree ————————— 58
  Early Snow in the High Country – 62
  Azaleas ————————— 68

Other Embellishments to Try 74
  Gathered Bushes and Shrubs — 74
  Microwave Wrinkles ———— 74
  Couched Trees ——————— 76

Putting It All Together ——— 77
  Selecting a Scene —————— 77
  Enlarging a Photo ————— 78

Words of Encouragement —— 79

Suggested Reading ———— 79

Supply Sources ——————— 80

About the Author ————— 80

Original Drawings ———— 81

Introduction

I have always enjoyed Mother Nature's shows and changing displays. As a fine arts student, it was a great pleasure to paint "on location." Growing up on a 200-acre farm in Minnesota, one of the biggest joys was being outdoors, planting things and watching them grow. The color changes in fall and winter and the "briskness" in the air have always been a source of exhilaration and inspiration to me.

Doing my landscaping with fabrics (instead of trowels, rakes, and hoes) has developed during the past ten years. In 1985, I attended a quilt show—mostly because it was held in a historic mansion I wanted to see. I came away thinking that someone should make a quilt of the mansion, which is a beautiful old house built around 1740. Guess who that someone was? At that time, I had no knowledge of quilting—grain lines, templates, ¼" seams—or for that matter, what kind of fabric should be used. Fortunately, I was comfortable with my sewing machine.

That first landscape took nearly three-and-a-half years to complete. I had to invent methods as I went along. Since I'm inclined to look for the easy way to do things, I think it took longer to invent the methods than it did to do the sewing. And the methods I came up with for that first quilt turned out to be anything but easy. I had very limited exposure to quilts and quilting, and no idea at all about how a quilt should be made. My ignorance turned out to be both a blessing (if I had known how much I had to learn, I might never have dared to start) and a curse (as I struggled with making the patterns and sewing the design).

I drew the first landscape full size on freezer paper, then cut the pattern apart, one section at a time, to use as templates. It never occurred to me that I should either (a) draw on the shiny side of the paper or (b) reverse the drawing. I pressed the first few pieces to the right side of the fabric and sewed them together.

Then I decided it would be easier to sew along the seam line if the paper were on the back side of the fabric. That way, it would be on top when I was stitching. I sewed a section together this way. It would have been a great idea if I had done either (a) or (b) above, but since I hadn't, it only resulted in reversing part of the picture, making it really difficult to get the sections to fit together. I was so ignorant of quilting, I had the quilt nearly finished before I figured out why I was having a problem.

By then, it was too late to do anything except continue to struggle; since I hadn't made a copy of my original drawing on freezer paper and it was now cut apart, I couldn't duplicate the problem sections without starting over. That experience led to developing the idea for "Master" and "Construction" patterns presented in "Basic Method" on pages 12–16. It was the first of many major learning experiences I would have while working on that piece.

The result, however, was worth all the pain. I donated it to the Friends of Belair, the committee raising funds to restore and refinish the mansion. The quilt is currently shown at events held by the Friends to raise money for restoration and will hang in the mansion when restoration is complete.

Though that first landscape pleased me (and I was honored to know it will hang in the mansion), I knew there had to be an easier way to do it—one that wouldn't take three-and-a-half years to complete.

This book presents the easy way. The basic component is string piecing: sewing narrow strips of fabric to a paper construction pattern. This method has been the basis for my landscapes since the first project.

In my classes, the only prerequisite is that the students be comfortable with their sewing machines. Most students are able to transform their 14" x 17" landscapes from master pattern to pieced (or nearly pieced) top in one six-hour session.

Designing the Quilt

Inspiration for my landscapes comes in many ways. Sometimes it is a desire to preserve in fabric a wonderful old building. It may be a magazine picture or a sketch I've done of a scene that particularly moved me. I have used black-and-white newspaper photos as well (they are really good source material because the lights and darks are easy to see and translate to fabric). The "Winter Sun" quilt on page 32 was inspired by a piece of Mickey Lawler's beautiful hand-painted Sky-Dye™ fabrics.

"But, I can't draw!" you say? For this method, drawing like a master artist is not necessary. The first project, "Sunset" (see pages 12–27), walks you through the basic method, showing you step by step how to place the shapes. All you really need to do is see the shapes and place them on paper. Your fabrics will do the rest, with help from a few fun-to-do embellishments.

I've also included master patterns for six small projects focusing on embellishment techniques, for those of you who do not want to design your own patterns right away.

To get the most from this book, read the text first, then go back and try the projects. Materials are listed in "Supplies and Materials" on pages 6–11, but you are by no means limited to the ones I have listed. Part of the fun of this method is the freedom to experiment. If a fabric, thread, tool, or technique strikes you as perfect for the mood you want to create, try it—it's probably just right.

The only rule in my classes and this book is there are no mistakes. There may be learning experiences and lots of serendipity, but no mistakes. So, experiment and enjoy.

Supplies and Materials

Fabrics

Cottons are best for piecing backgrounds.

Just as a painter uses pigments and brushes to create landscapes, a quilter uses fabrics and sewing tools. Both artists make representations of their chosen subject and convey ideas and feelings about the subject to the viewer.

Fabric has a built-in tactile quality that pigments lack. Use this tactile quality to your advantage when the texture is exactly what you need to convey your idea. Fabric can also challenge you to stretch your skills, to add just the right thread or embellishment to complete the statement.

With paint, mixing colors to get the right hue is easy—combining red and yellow to make orange, for example. In fabric, that same orange can be achieved by placing red and yellow next to each other, by "drawing" on the fabric with colored threads, letting the eye do the mixing, or by using fabric paints or dyes.

When I started making landscapes, I looked for small prints (but not calicoes) or tone-on-tone fabrics that reflected the colors and values of the scene I wanted to make. I rarely use solid-colored fabrics, feeling that they lack texture (although I have seen some beautiful scenes done by other people using solid fabrics).

Building my palette is a great excuse to go fabric shopping. When I realized I was hooked on landscape quilts, I began buying small pieces of fabrics, such as fat quarters (18" x 22") and fat eighths (9" x 22") that reminded me of sky, water, seasons or times of day, trees, grass, and buildings. Now, I choose fabrics for the reverse side as well as the front—it is often the perfect value for a design. It is really convenient to have exactly the color and value I need already on my shelf when I'm ready to start a new piece.

I use cottons for string piecing the background sections. Since these quilts will not be washed, other fabrics can be used as well. It's more important to keep the weight of the fabrics similar than to match the fiber content. For example, a denim-weight fabric pieced next to an organdy-weight fabric can cause problems, such as bubbles and sags in the finished work, even though both are cotton. The lighter-weight material stretches differently than the heavier one. However, organdy-weight fabric is great for overlays.

As I try different embellishment techniques, my fabric selection expands. My collection currently includes coarsely textured fabrics (content unknown, but similar to a lightweight burlap in texture) for painting and then fringing to make grasses and weeds. I also like to keep a selection of nylon tulle and fine tulles for overlays, and some glitzy pearlescent organzas and lamés for water reflections and snow-capped mountains.

Select fabrics by texture as well as by color. Printed cottons are available in designs that look like water, sky, stones, grasses, bricks, and nearly anything you can imagine. New fabrics come out almost daily, so visit your quilt shop regularly.

In addition to the textures that appear in printed fabric, consider using fabrics such as burlap, corduroy, or velveteen for a plowed field or a night scene. Napped fabrics shift slightly in color and value when oriented in different directions. This feature can be used to advantage in some scenes.

Rough fabrics that fray easily make great weeds or haystacks. A crinkled cotton in a neutral beige looks like a granite cliff when it is in a landscape. Drapery and upholstery shops have interesting textured fabrics and sometimes will sell (or give away) their out-dated sample books.

Color

It's important to collect a wide range of colors, values, and textures in your fabrics. For me, the scene I want to make determines the color selection. I tend to work intuitively, selecting colors, values, and textures as I go. It is useful, though, to have some basic color knowledge.

Color has four properties: hue, value, intensity, and temperature. These properties are defined below.

Hue—the color's name, such as red, yellow, blue.

Value—the lightness or darkness of a color relative to its surrounding colors. Shades are pure colors mixed with black. Tints are pure colors mixed with white.

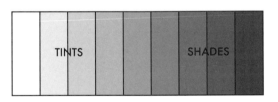

Value Scale

A color can be the lightest value in one fabric grouping and the darkest in another.

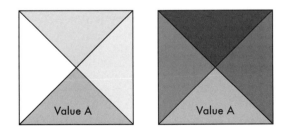

Intensity—the strength or saturation of a color. Pure color is the most intense; some colors, such as reds, oranges, and yellows, appear more intense than others. A grayed or muted color is also called a "tone." When placed next to black, all colors appear to be more intense than they appear when lying next to each other. The complement of a color (the color lying opposite on the color wheel) also enhances its intensity when placed side by side.

Temperature—the warmth or coolness of a color. This is useful to set the scene for particular times of the year, times of the day, weather conditions, or moods. Warm colors include red, orange, and yellow: the colors of fire and sunshine. Cool colors include blue, green, and violet: the colors of grass, sky, and water. Our perception of temperature is relative, depending upon a color's surrounding hues and whether the color is pure or toned, tinted or shaded. In a cool scene of blue and green, red-violet will be the warmest hue. The same red-violet will be the coolest hue next to the orange and scarlet of fall. Test this for yourself by placing swatches of red-violet next to swatches of blue and green, then next to orange and scarlet.

Color Manipulation—Like temperature, value and intensity are relative; that is, they are affected by whatever is placed next to them. When you look at a scene and a color looks wrong or out of place, it is usually because one of these variables is not in

Use novelty yarns and glitzy fabrics, such as organzas and tulles, for special effects.

harmony with its neighbors. You may have the perfect hue, but it is too dark, too intense, too hot, or too cool. Try using the reverse side of the fabric if a lighter value or less intense color is needed. Or, try changing neighboring hues to one of different intensity. In my own work, the hardest variable to work with is intensity. I'm drawn to very intense colors, and they tend to stray into most of my pieces.

Sometimes, I can keep intense color in a pale, toned scene by repeating the color in more than one spot. In "Winter Sun" (page 32), the intense orange of the sun threatened to overpower the picture. By repeating it in the small, round cabin window, I restored the balance, and the picture worked well.

Adjust value by using the reverse of a fabric, using overlays, or by "painting" with thread. The shadowed area of the large mountain in "Early Snow in the High Country" (page 62) includes thread painting to control value. Try changing adjacent fabrics to increase or decrease contrast in value. Or, try repeating the value that looks out of place.

Additional ways of manipulating color include shading, toning, or tinting fabrics by painting, overdyeing, or bleaching.

Shades—pure color mixed with black

Tones—grayed or muted color

Tint—white added to a color

Color research has provided some clues as to how colors affect moods. Hot colors tend to raise the blood pressure, pulse, and breathing rates—they stimulate. Pure red is the most intense of the hot colors. (Auto insurance surveys report that more accidents occur to red cars. It is not known whether this shows the owners are more aggressive and thus choose red cars, or whether other drivers are responding to the "red flag at the bull" effect.) Orange is said to increase the appetite, and yellow is used to stimulate mental processes.

Cool colors slow down body functions. This is a calming effect unless taken to extremes when depression (I've got the blues) can be the result. Clear greens are often considered healing.

Color symbolism is not the same worldwide. In the United States, white is a color for brides, indicating purity and innocence.

In India, white is the color of mourning. In Russia, the words for red and beauty are the same. In the United States, red is a passionate color and is used for both anger and love ("seeing red" or sending a red heart for a Valentine). Purple has long been considered a color for royalty ("born to the purple"), likely due to the fact that purples were once so costly that only the nobility could afford them. At one time, it was actually a crime for commoners to possess anything purple.

Nature makes good use of all colors. Most of the year, greens, blues, browns, and ochres are the dominant colors. We have occasional flashes of brilliant, intense colors at sunrise, at sunset, in fall foliage, and in the accents of bright flowers. Nature's colors, however, are most often restful, calm, cool colors.

For landscape work, intensive color-wheel study is not necessary, but it is a useful reference tool. (See color wheel opposite.)

Generally speaking, nature's harmonies are analogous (made of colors lying side by side on the color wheel). Try making an entire piece using just blues and greens, with a tint of blue serving as the sky, gray blue or gray green tones as distant hills, and dark shades of blue or green as trees and foliage.

For sunset or sunrise, use the analogous colors red, yellow, and orange, with their tints in the lightest areas and their shades in the darker areas. Sunsets are more intense than sunrises, and the light of high noon lessens contrasts as everything is washed in brilliant sunlight.

You can't put too many fabrics in a landscape; the variety of prints adds life to the picture as long as the hues, values, and intensities are right. In landscapes, colors in the foreground are more intense, gradually becoming bluer and fading as they recede into the distance.

Spring includes many clear tints of yellow-green and blue. Early summer colors are pure colors, with lots of bright greens, clear blue skies, and flowers in bloom. Midsummer colors are more muted, as the heat creates a haze and begins to turn the bright colors of early summer into tones.

The artist can use hues from most of the color wheel for a scene depicting the brilliant rusts, golds, oranges, and scarlets of autumn's display, but many of the colors will be shades instead of tints. (See bottom diagram at right.) Winter, especially in snow country, has a drama all its own. Use pale tones of blue, lavender, and pink for both the sky and the reflections in the snow.

Go outside and observe the changing colors of the seasons. Even the color of the sky changes from one season to the next—a clear, bright blue in spring and fall, a hazier blue in the summer, and often a lavender cast in winter. Make color notes as you observe. These notes will help in selecting colors and values for your quilted landscapes.

Joen Wolfrom has written an excellent section on general color notes for landscapes in her book *Landscapes and Illusions* (C & T Publishing). There are a number of other books available with good discussions of color, value, and harmony. Refer to the reading list on page 79 for other books.

My personal theory is that any colors will work well together if they relate to the mood I want to set and if the values and intensities are correct for my scene. Most of all, I think playing with color is fun. Experiment and enjoy as you learn about color.

Fabric Preparation

I no longer prewash most fabrics. I like the way the sized fabric handles. Shrinkage will not be a problem, since these are wall quilts and won't be washed. If a color is especially intense, I may wet a small piece and lay it on a paper towel to check for "bleeding." If it bleeds, I prewash or find a substitute. The best reason of all for not prewashing is that I don't need to iron the fabrics before I use them. I hate that step! It takes away time I could spend working on my design.

There is no need for a great deal of precision in cutting, since you will rarely use more than a small segment of a strip at a time. The construction pattern removes the need for matching the corners and points we usually work with in piecework. For small quilts (14" x 20" or less), I cut cotton fabrics into strips ⅝" to 1¼" wide. For larger quilts, I may include strips up to 1¾" wide.

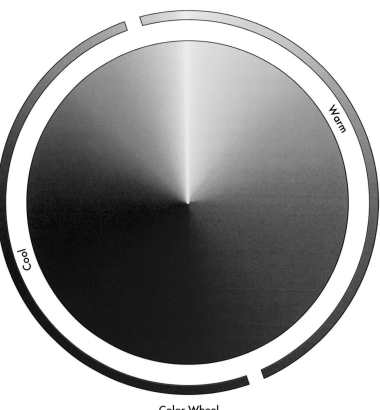

Color Wheel

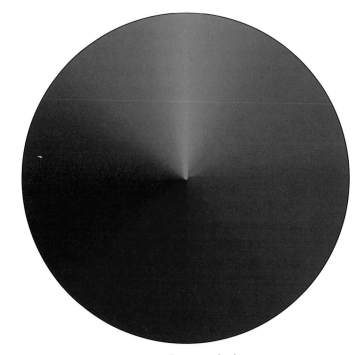

Autumn's hues are shades.

I cut scraps that look like parts of a landscape into short strips too. I store them in clear-plastic stacking boxes, sorted by theme—sunset, bright sky, night, grasses, etc. I don't cut my nets, glitzy fabrics, and other special fabrics until I'm ready to use them.

Sewing Machine

My machine is a Pfaff® 1472; however, any machine with a small stitch setting (16 to 20 stitches/inch) will do nicely for the piecing. Having a machine with a zigzag stitch and feed dogs that drop is convenient for free-motion embroidery and quilting (although I have a friend who covers the feed dogs and does free-motion work with her Singer® Featherweight—see "Quilting" on pages 22–23). A machine with a blanket stitch or blind hemstitch is nice for working with pieced appliqué. (See the pieced appliqué tree foliage in the photo of "Fall Tree" on page 58. The instructions for making the quilt are on pages 59–61.)

Most importantly, keep the machine clean and oiled. Each time you change the bobbin, brush away the lint that has accumulated. Use the brush that comes with your machine, or use a small nylon artists' brush. Oil your machine according to the manufacturer's specifications.

A darning foot and a walking foot are two accessories you will find useful for making quilted landscapes. If you do not have either of these feet, check with your sewing machine dealer. Both can be purchased for most machines.

Be sure to change the needle when you start a new project. I use size 11/12 for piecing and change to a machine-embroidery needle or a size 14 jeans or topstitch needle for free-motion quilting with metallic threads.

Normal tension settings are fine for most piecing, but when I use metallic threads, I loosen the top tension. On my machine, the setting for normal is between 3 and 5; loosen it for metallics. Experiment to find the setting that works best on your machine.

The combination of a lower setting with a larger needle helps to prevent fraying and breaking when using metallics and other fine machine-embroidery threads. I also use a liquid silicone product (Sewer's Aid®) liberally on the spool of thread before I begin to sew with metallic thread.

Thread

I use neutral gray or off-white thread for most of my piecing. Usually, I use J. & P. Coats® Dual Duty, a cotton-covered polyester thread. For quilting and free-motion work, I use rayon or cotton machine-embroidery threads and metallics for details, invisible nylon smoke-colored thread to quilt the darker areas, and clear invisible thread for the lighter areas. Sulky®, DMC®, and Mez are my favorite machine-embroidery threads. Madeira and Sulky are my favorite metallics. I will try any thread I can fit through the needle's eye.

When shopping for invisible thread, beware! Don't buy the cheap stuff that feels like fishing line. Purchase the fine-textured kind, even though it costs a bit more. The heavier monofilament threads will show on most pieces, they are more difficult to work with, and the ends tend to create a scratchy area on the quilt.

Match the bobbin thread to the backing fabric for quilting and embroidery, and to the top thread for piecing. Recently, I've been experimenting with Janome's™ bobbin thread for free-motion work, using metallic threads and the lighter-weight embroidery threads on top. I find using this thread in the bobbin really helps cut down on the fraying and/or breaking of the top threads. Janome's thread does have two drawbacks: it is hard to find in my area, and I can only get it in white. Some embellishments require elastic thread for the bobbin.

Paper, Pencils, and Carbon Paper

Pattern-making supplies are inexpensive and readily available in office-supply or art-supply shops. I prefer artists' newsprint for pattern making. This is a lightweight paper that is easy to remove after sewing, yet sturdy enough to take erasures and lots of handling during the piecing process. It comes in pads of assorted sizes. My favorite size is 14" x 17". If I need a larger pattern, I just tape several sheets together.

I use a No. 2 pencil for drawing and two pencils of two different colors for marking the patterns. I use Berol™ colored pencils, but any brand of pencil that will keep a sharp point is fine.

I also use 8½" x 11" typing carbons for tracing the master pattern onto the construction pattern.

Paints, Inks, and Markers

For embellishments, fabric paints, inks, and markers are useful. I especially like Versatex™ inks for a semitransparent wash of color and Versatex fabric paints for opaque painting. (See "Supply Sources" on page 80.) I recently started experimenting with Lumiere™ and Neopaque™ fabric paints.

In a pinch for the right color, I will also use the fabric paints sold in craft stores, and/or the tubes of acrylic paints artists use. Acrylic paints sold in craft stores can be very stiff when they dry. With these paints, use a light touch and work in layers to get the desired color, letting the paint dry between layers to minimize the stiffness.

Heat-set all of these paints with your iron, following the manufacturer's directions.

I suggest buying sampler paint sets to get started. Basic colors I have found useful include blue, red, brown, yellow, white, and navy blue.

I use Y & C Fabric Mate fabric markers. I like the fine-point brush tip because the point is great for line work and the side of the tip is perfect for shading. I also like Niji markers. The paint doesn't seem to dry out if it is kept tightly covered when not in use. Both markers are available in a wide range of colors. You can purchase them individually or in sets.

Choose inexpensive, ¼"- to ½"-wide flat nylon brushes. Start saving the white plastic lids from three-pound coffee cans and whipped-topping or margarine containers to use as throw-away palettes for your inks and paints.

Miscellaneous Supplies

You will need a rotary cutter, a see-through acrylic ruler as a cutting guide, and a self-healing cutting mat. You will also need sharp scissors for cutting fabric, paper scissors, water-soluble glue stick, ¾"-long appliqué or sequin pins, 1"-long safety pins for basting (about 30 pins for most quilts), a steam iron, and an ironing board or pad. (Please note: I didn't forget seam rippers. This is one technique where you won't need them.)

For embellishments, choose a spring-type machine-embroidery hoop. This type of hoop has a plastic outer ring and metal inner ring and comes in sizes from 3" to 10" in diameter. Purchase the largest size available. This type of hoop makes it easier to get the fabric as tight as a drum. I have tried the wooden hoops with screw tighteners but found it difficult to get the fabric tight enough. If, however, you already have a hoop you feel comfortable with, there is no need to purchase a new one for these projects.

ARTIST'S TIP

Using ¾"-long pins is critical to successfully sewing the sections together.

Basic Method

Sunset

Finished size:
19" × 16"

The method discussed on the following pages is the basis for making all of the landscapes in this book. By adding embellishments to this basic method, you can create your own personalized scenes. (See "Embellishing the Landscape" on pages 42–43 and the embellishment projects beginning on page 44.) I suggest you read through the basic method section to become familiar with the process. Then go back and create your first project by following the steps to make your master and construction patterns and sew the quilt—a sunset reflected in the water.

Sunset by Joan Blalock, 1992, Bowie, Maryland, 26"x 20¼". This quilt is a larger variation of the project quilt.

MATERIALS
44"-wide fabric

In addition to the general supplies listed on pages 6 – 11, you will need the following:

¾ yd. total assorted cotton strips, ⅞" to 1½" wide, in pinks, purples, yellows, oranges, blue grays, and dark navy blue or purple-on-black prints for sky, water, and hills

20" x 22" rectangle of fabric for backing

20" x 22" rectangle of batting

⅓ yd. print for binding

Variegated metallic thread

Invisible monofilament thread

Making the Master Pattern
Drawing Your Own Pattern

The following instructions take you through the steps for drawing your own master pattern. If you do not wish to start this way, enlarge the original drawing for "Sunset" on page 81 or one of the other original drawings on pages 82–87.

1. On a horizontally oriented piece of newsprint, draw a horizon line across the page from edge to edge. Draw a low horizon line if you are emphasizing a dramatic sky, or a high horizon line if your emphasis will be on the land. Avoid putting the horizon line exactly in the center. A center horizon line causes the picture to be too static so the eye bounces back and forth from top to bottom, without finding a place to rest.

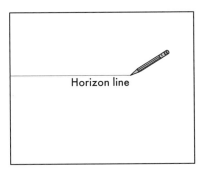

2. Add general shapes of land masses, trees, bodies of water, buildings, and any major features in the sky, such as the clouds, sun, or moon. Do not worry about details; just put in the general shapes. When you are satisfied with your landscape, label it "Master." It is also helpful to label any major segments of land, sky, or water.

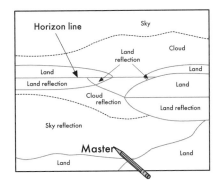

3. Draw cutting lines in the sky and water areas. Use cutting lines to divide the pattern into convenient sections for sewing. *Cutting the pattern along these lines prevents the need to change colors later when you are sewing the strips together and helps avoid difficult set-in seams.*

When drawing the cutting lines, start with the steepest, most vertical edge of your cloud shape and draw the first cutting line along this edge, extending the line to the top of the picture from the edge of the cloud.

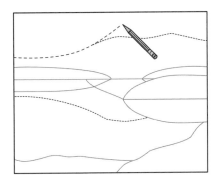

ARTIST'S TIP

The gentler the curve, the easier your piecing will be.

4. Above the horizon line, draw the remaining cutting lines roughly parallel to the first line, following the same general curves. Remember to take the cue for drawing cutting lines from the outlines of the cloud and land shapes. The sky is reflected in reverse in bodies of water, so draw your cutting lines below the horizon (in the water) as mirror images of the cutting lines above.

For this picture, cutting lines are drawn in the sky and water only; extend the cutting lines just to the edges of the land. The edges of the land shapes will serve as cutting lines between land/sky and land/water areas.

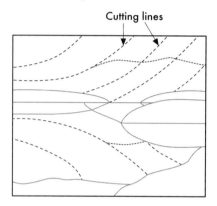

Cutting lines

Note: *You may choose to draw more (or fewer) cutting lines in your master pattern than those shown in the illustration. This is fine. The cutting lines are an aid to make the sewing easier, so put them where they will help you.*

Enlarging the Pattern

The following steps show you how to enlarge a design using one of the gridded original drawings on pages 81–87.

1. On a 14" x 17" piece of newsprint, draw a 2" x 2" grid. The lines represent the grid drawn on the original drawing.

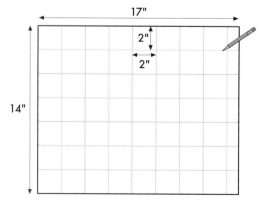

2. Choose a line on the original drawing. On the newsprint grid, mark the approximate spot where the line crosses the corresponding smaller grid.

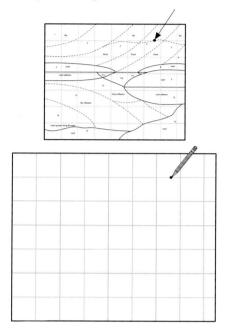

3. Mark another spot where the same line on the original drawing crosses another grid line. Referring to the original, sketch a similar line between points on the newsprint.

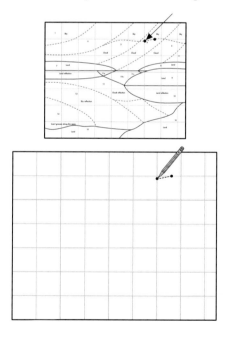

4. Continue marking and connecting points on the grid to make a master pattern. Next, follow step 3 of "Drawing Your Own Pattern" on page 13, then follow the steps for "Making the Construction Pattern" below.

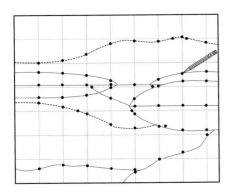

Making the Construction Pattern

The construction pattern is an identical pattern to the master pattern that you will cut apart to use as pattern pieces. If you are wondering, "Why make a second drawing?" the project in the photograph above right shows what happened the time I didn't follow my own advice.

Notice that the bottom section doesn't fit with the top. Yes, you guessed it! I cut up my master pattern instead of taking the time to make a second (construction) pattern. I was in a rush to complete the quilt as a construction sample for a class and I sewed the lower section to the wrong side of the paper. If I had made both master and construction patterns, I could have simply remade the lower section. Repairing my mistake wasn't possible. I saved my "construction module" as an example of what not to do—*never* cut up the master pattern!

1. Using carbon paper, trace your master pattern onto a second sheet of newsprint. This will be your construction pattern. I use several sheets of carbon paper, side by side, covering the entire picture. This eliminates shifting. If you use only one sheet of carbon paper, move it carefully from place to place to prevent the drawings from shifting.

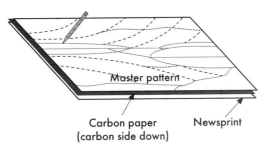

Master pattern

Carbon paper (carbon side down)   Newsprint

2. Set aside the master pattern. To make hash marks on both sides of the pattern, place the carbon paper, *carbon side up*, under your construction pattern. With a colored pencil, make hash marks across all cutting lines and all areas where the land meets the sky and/or water. Make the hash marks about $1/2$" long and 1" apart (closer on tight curves). Be sure the marks cross the lines. The hash marks are very important for matching pieces when you begin to sew (similar to notches on a dress pattern). Mark the top and bottom points of tight curves.

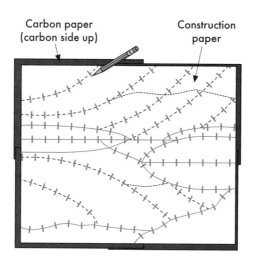

Carbon paper (carbon side up)   Construction paper

Note: *Do not make hash marks on the edges of reflections or clouds, unless they lie on a cutting line. These edges will be string-pieced within the section. Use hash marks only for matching seam lines between cut sections as shown at right.*

3. Remove the carbons. On the front of the construction pattern with a second, different-colored pencil, draw straight lines from side to side, parallel to the horizon line. Use another colored pencil for this—one that will catch your attention as you sew. Draw these lines about 1" apart through the sky and water areas *(not the land areas).*

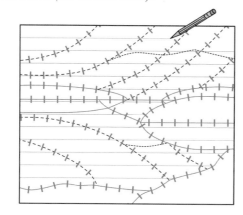

Use these lines as guides when string piecing the sky and water strips, to keep them parallel to the horizon line. They are not meant to be used as sewing lines, although you may occasionally sew a strip along one

ARTIST'S TIP

Skies are normally lightest at the horizon line and gradually darken toward the "top." Rising storms or partly cloudy skies are sometimes exceptions to this rule.

of them. Without these guidelines, it is easy to lose the horizontal orientation on the curved sections of the sky and water, creating a chevron effect.

The land areas are sewn later, following the shape of the land as a guide instead of horizontal lines. You may draw guidelines on the land if you like, following the slope of the land, but they are not necessary.

At this point, your construction drawing will look like a confusing mess. Trust me; the reasons for this become clear as you sew.

Assembly

String Piecing

1. Number the sections on your patterns. Cut one sky section from the construction pattern along the marked cutting lines. In general, the sky sets the tone for landscapes, so sew it first.

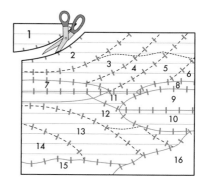

2. Lay the first strip of fabric right side up at the top of the pattern segment with about ¼" of fabric extending beyond the paper. A dab of glue stick will help hold it in place.

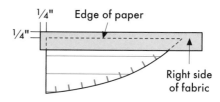

¼" Edge of paper
¼"
Right side of fabric

3. Set your machine for 16 to 20 stitches to the inch. This small stitch perforates the paper and makes it easy to remove when the picture is complete.

4. Lay the second strip face down on top of the first and sew the strips together, through the paper, with a ⅛"- to ³/₁₆"-wide seam allowance (or trim to that width if you are more comfortable with wider seams).

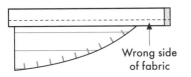

Wrong side of fabric

5. Flip and firmly finger-press the second strip. Make sure the strips lie flat before you add the next strip; otherwise, you may get little bubbles in the pieced top when you remove the paper. If you have trouble finger pressing the seams flat, use the iron set on a steam setting. (The steam also weakens the paper and aids in easy removal when the quilt top is complete.)

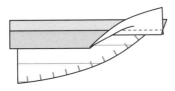

Note: *Throughout the book, when the instructions call for ironing, iron with steam, vigorously, as you would clothing. If you see the term "press," use a dry iron, lifting the iron from place to place the way you normally do for quilting, rather than sliding it.*

6. Continue adding strips and finger pressing until the paper is covered with fabric and the fabric extends approximately ¼" past the edges all around.

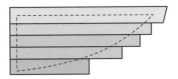

Note: *Sometimes two different areas meet in a diagonal line within a section, such as in the cloud and sky section in the illustration below.*

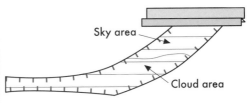

Sky area

Cloud area

To avoid difficult piecing, first sew the widest strip of sky fabric (1½" wide) to the pattern. Iron the fabric strip over the pattern.

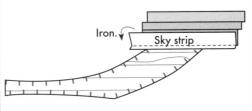

Iron.

Sky strip

Next, sew the widest strip of cloud fabric along the angled sky/cloud line on the pattern. (The first strip of sky fabric will cover the line on the pattern. Lift up the strip to see the placement line for the first cloud strip.) Make sure the strip extends to the edge of the pattern. Trim the sky fabric, flip, and iron.

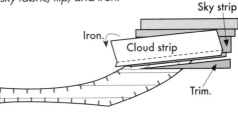

Sky strip

Iron.

Cloud strip

Trim.

Add the next strip of cloud fabric, angling it parallel to the guidelines, and trim the excess fabric from the previous strip.

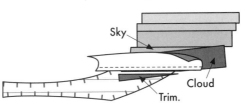

Sky

Cloud

Trim.

Sometimes, if your second angled strip is too narrow, you will need a third angled strip to follow the horizontal guidelines again.

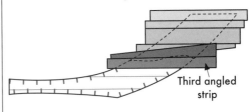

Third angled strip

7. String-piece the water sections in the same manner as the sky sections.

8. Iron each completed section. Trim fabric strips to ¼" beyond the paper on all edges.

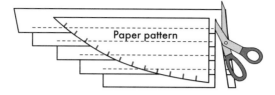

9. Lay completed sections in place on the master pattern. Having sections in place as you work will help you judge what colors and values come next in your picture.

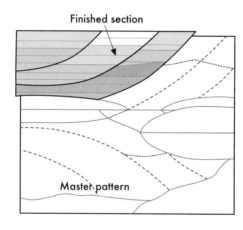

10. When you come to the land areas, you will no longer be following guides parallel to the horizon. Instead, follow the slope of the land as you add strips. I've drawn a few lines on Land Section 7 in the illustration below to show the slope for strip placement; draw your own lines first or stitch strips, following the general contour of the land. String-piece all sections.

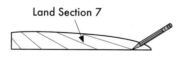

11. Beginning with the pattern for the hill farthest in the distance, place the first strip right side up, making sure that there will be enough fabric to include seam allowances.

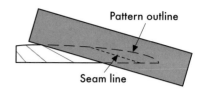

12. Place the second strip on top of the first strip, right sides together. Flip the strip to make sure it will cover the pattern, then stitch.

Note: *It is not necessary to cut strips to match the shape on the pattern. Instead, "skew" them as you sew. Take a wider seam allowance where you want the piece to be narrow and taper the width of the seam allowance toward the opposite end of the piece, where you want the strip to be wide.*

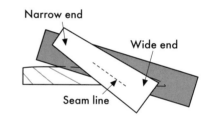

13. Trim the extra seam allowance before adding the next strip. Repeat for the remaining strips. Strip-piece Land Sections 8, 9, and 10, working from the farthest hill toward the nearest.

Joining Sections

1. Sew Sections 1–6 together in numerical order. Using ¾"-long appliqué/sequin pins, pin two sections, right sides together, by matching the hash marks. Longer pins skew the bottom layer so the pieces don't fit together. Do not attempt to match horizontal seam lines. Insert each pin through both pieces, perpendicular to the edge of the fabric and *just touching the edge of the paper on both sides.* Take a small "bite," bringing the point of the pin out through the paper pattern. Clip curves to the edge of the paper, if necessary, to fit sections together more easily.

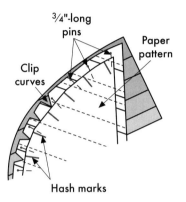

Note: *It is usually easier to begin pinning at pointed edges of the patterns. Make sure to align both edges of the paper as you pin. Take care not to let the section underneath slide, or the two sections will not fit together, creating bubbles or poor alignment in the sewn piece.*

2. Set the machine for 12 to 15 stitches to the inch and sew the completed sections together, stitching along the edge of the paper. Sew Sections 7 and 8 to Sections 1–6.

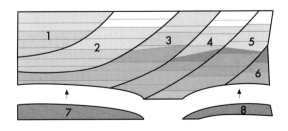

Note: *Iron the seam allowances toward the section that appears closest to the viewer to make the section look like it is in front. Iron the seam allowances within sky and water sections open or toward cloud shapes.*

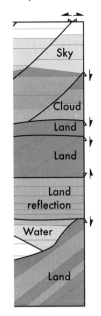

3. Sew Section 9 to Section 10. Sew Sections 11a and 11c to Section 11b. Then sew Section 9/10 to Section 11a/b/c.

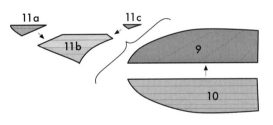

4. Join Sections 12, 13, and 14 in numerical order, then sew Section 12/13/14 to the unit made in step 3.

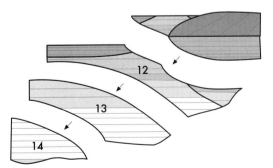

Basic Method

5. Join the land/water unit made in step 4 to the sky/cloud unit made in step 2.

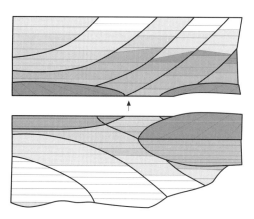

6. For the foreground hill, add a strip of fabric "grass" to vary the texture and provide some dimension. Make the grass by using a 2"- to 3"-wide strip of one of the fabrics you used for the hill. Fringe it by pulling out threads along the crosswise grain on one edge of the strip (the way we did in grade-school art classes for Mother's Day napkins). Leave a ⅜"-wide strip of unfringed fabric to attach to the quilt. Cut across this fringed strip to make sections if desired.

3/8"

ARTIST'S TIP

Sometimes I paint a coarse fabric first in the dark color I need and then fringe it. Versatex inks are nice for this; they don't stiffen the fabric. I mix the paints on the palette or directly on moistened fabric. These paints are so user friendly that my young grandsons often do this part—they love helping.

7. With right sides up, place one or more sections of grass on the water section, then pin Land Section 15 face down on top. Pin or baste, then sew the seam through all three layers. Press seam allowances toward the hill.

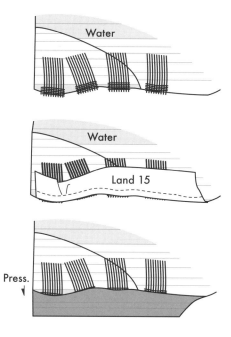

ARTIST'S TIP

To make the grass stay in place after the quilt is complete, slide a piece of cardboard between the grass sections and the quilt; spray heavily with extra-firm hair spray.

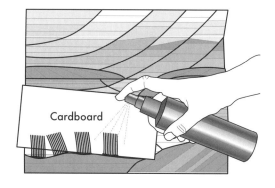

8. Strip-piece and join Section 16 to the quilt, adding more grass if you like.

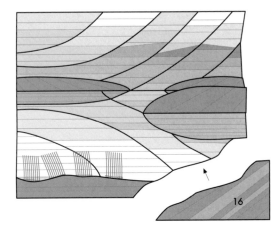

Preparing to Quilt

1. Iron the quilt top one more time with steam.

2. Carefully remove the paper from the back. The paper should be very easy to remove if you remembered to sew with 16 to 20 stitches per inch. If there are tiny pieces of paper left where seams join, don't be too concerned. Since this is a wall hanging, they will not be a problem.

3. Press, if needed, with a dry iron.

Note: *There are two methods for adding borders to this piece. If you wish to add the Skewed Log Cabin border, do not square up the quilt, but follow steps 5–9. If you prefer mitered borders, read through the instructions first and decide whether to add them now or after quilting. Instructions for making the Skewed Log Cabin borders are on pages 23–24. Instructions for making mitered borders are on pages 24–25.*

4. Measure through the middle and along the edges both horizontally and vertically. All horizontal measurements should be the same, and all vertical measurements should match. Make sure all corners are 90° (right-angle) corners.

If the measurements are different, square up the quilt by placing a Bias Square®, carpenter's T-square, or other square cutting guide in one corner of the quilt top. Mark the corner. Place a straight edge against the Bias Square. Remove the square and mark or trim along the straight edge. Repeat for the remaining corners.

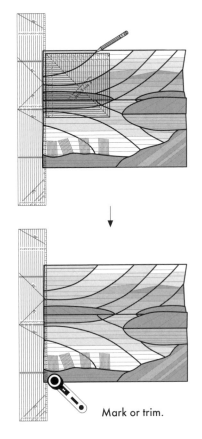

Mark or trim.

5. Press the backing fabric. Using masking tape, tape the fabric, right side down, to a tabletop. Start taping a the top edge, in the center. Next, tape at the center of the lower edge, stretching the fabric slightly as you go.

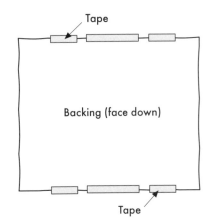

Tape

Backing (face down)

Tape

6. Tape the sides, again stretching slightly. Work out from the centers to the corners, smoothing and stretching as you work.

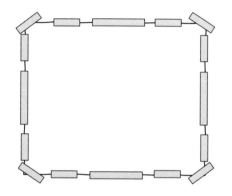

7. Layer the batting, then the quilt top, right side up, over the backing, centering and smoothing each layer in place.

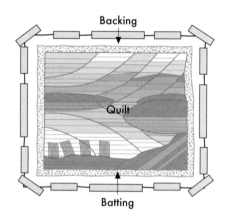

8. Pin with safety pins, first in a vertical row, then in a horizontal row, dividing the quilt into quadrants with the pins. Place pins no more than 3" apart. Continue pinning, filling in each quadrant so that you finish with a grid of safety pins.

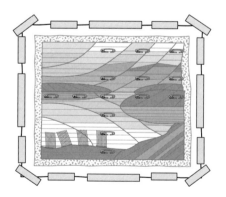

9. When the entire top is pinned, remove the masking tape.

Quilting

I do most of my quilting by machine, using free-motion techniques. To do this, I drop (or cover) the feed dogs and attach a darning foot or spring needle. Some older machines have an extra throat plate for this. A friend of mine tapes two pieces of template plastic over the feed dogs, leaving a space for the needle.

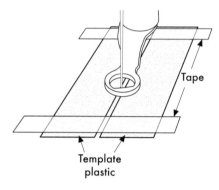

I seldom mark my quilting lines. Instead, I prefer to "draw" lines with machine stitches that will enhance the picture. If you think of the pieced landscape as the colored part of a painting, and the quilting lines as the outlines or drawing lines needed to clarify the scene, it may be easier to start.

If you have never tried free-motion machine quilting, make a sample square for practice, complete with backing and batting. Use fabrics and batting similar to those in the quilt and practice using both metallic thread and invisible, monofilament thread. For the bobbin, use all-purpose cotton thread or cotton-wrapped polyester thread that matches the backing fabric.

When using metallic thread, use machine-embroidery, Metafil®, or top-stitching needles (size 14). Set the machine at half speed (or sew very slowly if your machine doesn't have a half-speed setting) so the thread won't fray and break. Apply Sewer's Aid lubricant liberally to the spool of thread to keep fraying to a minimum.

Begin machine quilting by taking one stitch, then pulling the bobbin thread to the top of the quilt. Holding both thread ends to one side, take three or four stitches in place (or tiny short stitches). Trim thread ends and begin quilting.

Run the machine as fast as possible for the thread you are using and regulate the stitch length by moving the fabric slowly with your hands. The stitch length will even out once you develop a comfortable rhythm.

For those who prefer a more structured approach, refer to the illustration below for suggested quilting lines.

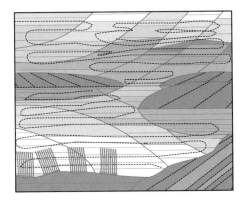

1. Starting with variegated metallic thread, quilt the water lines. Keep these lines horizontal. Remove the safety pins as you come to them. Where the water meets the distant hills, stitch three or four rows of quilting close together. This creates a realistic shoreline, separating the land from the water.

Note: *Enhance the illusion of distance by quilting the lines farther apart as you approach the middle and foreground areas.*

2. When the quilting for the water is complete, change the top thread to invisible smoke-colored monofilament thread and stitch the remaining quilting lines. Follow the contour of the land when quilting land or hill areas. Enhance the point where land meets sky or water by quilting in-the-ditch. For other areas, quilt across strips or between seams.

Adding the Borders
Skewed Log Cabin Borders

I developed the borders for "Sunset" accidentally when I omitted the step of squaring up the quilt. I guess I was too excited to see my finished work before layering and quilting. I realized after quilting the layers that the corners weren't square.

I used strips left over from string piecing. The strips were of irregular widths, and skewing them emphasized this irregularity.

1. Begin with the quilt that has not been squared after assembling and quilting. (Remember, I forgot to square it before I quilted it.) Instead, use a pencil and, with a light touch, mark a straight line around the edges of the quilt. The corners of the quilt will *not* be 90° angles. Use the line as a guide for the first round of log strips.

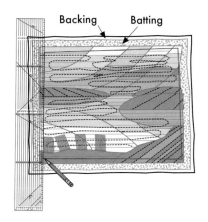

Backing   Batting

2. With right sides together, place the first strip at the left edge of the quilt so the edge just touches the line. Pin, then stitch the strip to the quilt top, batting, and backing. Flip and press.

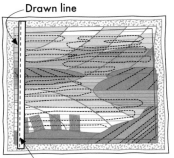

Drawn line

Stitching line

3. Repeat step 2 for the right edge of the quilt, then sew the top and bottom strips to the quilt, pressing after each addition.

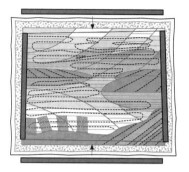

ARTIST'S TIP

If your leftover strips aren't long enough to reach from one edge of the quilt to the other, join a strip of one or more different fabrics to get the length you need.

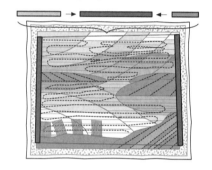

4. For borders 2 and 3, repeat steps 2 and 3, skewing the edges of the strips as you go, trimming excess, and pressing after adding each strip.

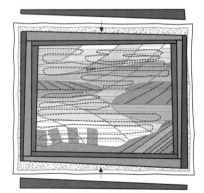

5. Square up the quilt, following the directions for squaring the quilt on page 21.

Mitered Borders

You can also make borders from 2"- to 3"- wide strips of a coordinating fabric and miter them at the corners. Attach these strips either before or after layering and quilting.

I like to leave 2" or 3" of extra batting and backing around the quilt and attach the borders through all layers *after* I quilt. This method often eliminates the need to do much quilting in the borders.

Note: *For quilts with multiple borders, cut each border strip, then sew them together into a unit and treat the unit as one border.*

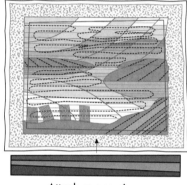

Attach as one piece.

1. Measure through the center of the quilt from top to bottom. To this measurement, add 2 times the width of the border (plus ½" for seam allowances) and add 1½" for a "fudge factor." Cut 2 side-border strips to this length. Repeat for the top and bottom borders.

For example, if the quilt measures 14" from the top to the bottom edges, and your finished border strips are 2" wide, cut the side-border strips 2½" x 19½".

$$14" + 2" + 2" + 1\frac{1}{2}" = 19\frac{1}{2}"$$

If the quilt measures 17" from side to side, cut the top and bottom border strips 2½" x 22½".

$$17" + 2" + 2" + 1\frac{1}{2}" = 22\frac{1}{2}"$$

2. Stitch all 4 borders to the quilt, starting and stopping ¼" from the edge of the quilt for each border.

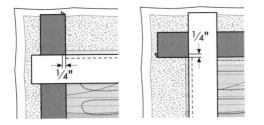

3. At the ironing board, press the seam allowances toward the borders. For each corner, place the quilt right side up and lay one strip out straight. Fold the adjacent strip under at a 45° angle, adjusting the fold until the two strips line up. Press and pin the fold.

Fold

If you are adding the borders before quilting:

Fold the quilt diagonally, right sides together, lining up the border strips at one corner. Fold seam allowances out of the way and pin along the crease. Pin along the edge of the borders so they remain aligned. Stitch along the crease, beginning where the seams meet.

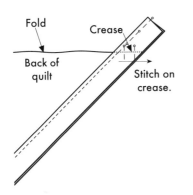

Fold

Crease

Back of quilt

Stitch on crease.

Trim the seam allowances to ¼" and press the seams open. Repeat for the remaining corners.

If you are adding the borders after quilting:

At each corner, fold and hand stitch the borders together along the miter, using a blind stitch. Stitch only the border fabrics; do not catch the batting or backing underneath. Flip the borders up and trim to within ¼" of the stitching.

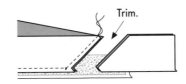

Trim.

If you prefer to use the machine, trim the excess fabric before stitching. Topstitch through all layers, along the miter.

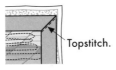

Topstitch.

If a border is puffier than the rest of the quilt and appears to need some quilting, machine quilt a straight line ½" from the quilt's outer edge, stopping and pivoting on the miter lines. Add another line of quilting ½" from the border's inner seam. This is usually enough to reduce the excess puffiness and makes the border look like a picture frame. For best results, use a walking foot on your machine.

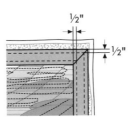

½"

½"

Adding the Binding

I like a narrow binding on a piece this small. On this quilt, it looks like another Log Cabin strip because of its narrow width.

1. Begin with the number of 1¾"- wide strips needed to go around the quilt. This will make a ¼"- wide finished binding. Join the strips end to end by placing the ends of the strips together at right angles (with right sides together) and sewing at a 45° angle. Trim seam allowances to ¼" wide. Press the seams open.

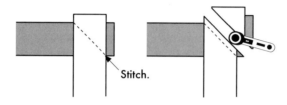

Stitch.

2. Fold the strip in half lengthwise, right side out. Press the strip to crease along the fold.

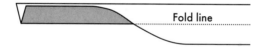

Fold line

3. Place the binding on the top of the quilt, midway between two corners, with all raw edges even. Attach the walking foot to your machine and begin stitching the binding, leaving a loose tail of binding about 2" long at the start. Use a ¼"-wide seam allowance. Stitch, stopping ¼" from the corner. Remove the quilt from the machine.

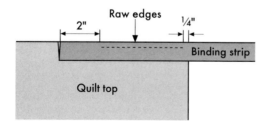

Raw edges

2"   ¼"

Binding strip

Quilt top

4. Fold the binding away from the quilt at a 90° angle, then fold down along the next edge, keeping the fold even with the top of the piece.

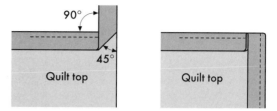

90°

45°

Quilt top

Quilt top

5. Begin stitching at the edge of the quilt. Sew the second side, again stopping ¼" from the corner, and repeat step 4. Repeat for the remaining sides. When you are within 2" of the beginning tail, stop sewing. Unfold and cut the beginning tail at a 45° angle, then fold the end under ¼".

6. Slide the end of the binding into the beginning until the two tails exactly fit the remaining space to be bound. Refold and align the raw edges; stitch the remaining distance.

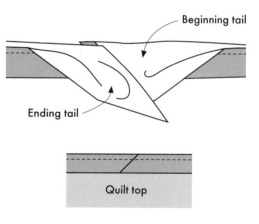

Beginning tail

Ending tail

Quilt top

7. Fold over to the back and hand stitch, using a blind stitch. As you come to each corner, fold the binding to form the miter; miters will form on the front as you turn the fabric.

Making a Hanging Sleeve

1. Cut an 8"-wide strip of backing fabric 1" shorter than the width of your quilt. With right sides together, fold in half lengthwise and stitch into a tube.

2. Hem both ends of the tube, turning under ¼" twice, concealing the raw edges. Turn right side out and press with the seam centered underneath the tube.

3. Attach to the back of the quilt by hand with blind stitching, being careful not to sew through to the front.

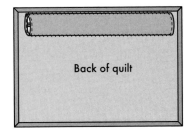

Back of quilt

Note: For small pieces (20" x 20" or less), where distortion from the weight of the piece will not be a factor, I have experimented with basting, then sewing the top of the sleeve to the quilt at the same time I attach the binding. This works fine for small pieces, and you only need to hand stitch the bottom edge of the sleeve this way.

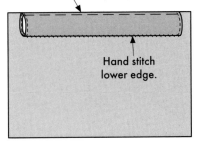

Baste sleeve to top edge of quilt.

Hand stitch lower edge.

On larger pieces, sleeves added with this technique look bad when the piece is hung. The rod pushes the sleeve up, causing it to show above the top, and pushes the binding forward so it resembles a tuck.

Gallery

The basic method uses the pattern I've taught in classes for the past four years. One of the most exciting things about the classes is seeing how different students interpret this pattern. As you look through the Gallery, take note of the basic-method quilts on pages 29–31. They are all made from the basic pattern, but how different they are!

Each artist made the scene her own. The women who made the quilts (while participating in the classes) are each at a different stage of quilting; some have been quilting for a very short time, some for years. For several individuals, this type of landscape quilt was a stretch from their usual styles. In fact, several women said, "I'm not an artist, I don't think I can do this." Looking at the finished pieces, I see that they are all artists.

As you look through the Gallery, study the pieces and see how different effects were accomplished. Then, as you work on the embellishing projects in the next section, refer to the Gallery to study how the artists used the embellishments. Most of all, I hope you enjoy the pieces as much as I enjoyed seeing them develop, and I hope they also inspire you to do your own "landscaping" with fabrics and thread.

Lac Lemon
*by Debra
Blaylock-Hanes,
1995,
Bowie, Maryland,
19" x 18".
Debra used glittery
tulle and organza
with chopped scraps
for this scene. She
also painted the tree
trunk with bleach.*

Colorado!
*by Florence E.
Marion,
1995,
Bowie, Maryland,
19" x 15½".
Flo said her
clouds looked like
mountains, so she let
them be mountains.
This piece includes
machine embroidery,
chopped scraps, and
tulle overlays. It
was a red-ribbon
winner in The
Southern Comforter's
1995 Show.*

Serenity
by Carol Hobbs,
1995,
Odenton, Maryland,
24" x 20".
Note Carol's
whimsical
embellishments—
ducks, textured
cattails, trees, and log
cabins add to the
scene for a fun quilt.

Tranquillity
by Barbara S. Bletch,
1995,
Hyattsville,
Maryland,
21½" x 19".
Barbara said her
cloud bank refused
to be clouds—so
they are mountains!
She notes that the
sun does not need
to be visible to
give the effect of a
sunrise or sunset.

Alaskan Sunset
by Phyllis Zwirko,
1995,
Glenn Dale,
Maryland,
21" x 19¾".
Phyllis used a
number of her
own hand-marbled
and tie-dyed fabrics
in this piece.
Pearlescent organza
creates the glacier.
Note the thread-
painted polar bear
carrying his dinner
across the ice.
Phyllis says this was
her first attempt at
thread painting.

Old Oak Tree
by Doris Amiss Rabey,
1995,
Hyattsville,
Maryland,
25¼" x 19½".
Doris added her
own techniques to the
basic string piecing
to create the oak
tree and foliage.

Winter Sun
by Joan Blalock,
1993,
Bowie, Maryland,
39" x 35½".
This piece includes
a painted cabin,
thread-painted
background trees, and
three-dimensional,
painted pine trees.

Morning
Breaks o'er
Foxhill Bridge
by Barbara Dolney,
1995,
Bowie, Maryland,
21¾" x 19¾".
Barbara has created
a lovely, soft morning
effect. She used tulle
to create the trees in
the background.
Note how the scene
continues in the
arches of the bridge.

*A View
from the Swing*
by Jane F. McKinley,
1995,
Upper Marlboro,
Maryland,
22" x 19".
An excellent use
of chopped scraps
suggests specific
flowers—iris, lilacs,
and delphiniums.
Jane made this piece
to commemorate
the view from the
porch swing at her
girlhood home.

*Beauty in My
Own Back Yard*
by Florence E. Marion,
1995,
Bowie, Maryland,
19" x 16".
This piece won a
blue ribbon in The
Southern Comforter's
1995 Challenge.
Metallic threads
were used for the
thread painting.

Chincoteague!
by Florence E. Marion,
1995,
Bowie, Maryland,
18" x 15".
Flo chose machine
appliqué and
thread painting to
embellish her quilt.

Lighthouse Point by Carol Hobbs, 1995, Odenton,
Maryland, 15" x 24". Rumpled fabrics, yarn, and lace
enabled Carol to create this quilt with a minimum of piecing.

Japanese Landscape by Doris Kirschbaum, 1995,
Greenbelt, Maryland, 19" x 22". Chopped scraps and tulle
overlays grace this interpretation of a Japanese postcard.

Old Abandoned Lighthouse
by Betty L. Russell, 1995, Bladensburg, Maryland, 19¾" x 19¼". Betty used a wonderful selection of fabrics to portray this old lighthouse. Orange thread painting in the water makes the piece glow.

New Jersey Sunrise
by Marion R. Wise, 1995, Bowie, Maryland, 23" x 21". This piece was inspired by the same New Jersey Travel and Tourism ad as "Old Abandoned Lighthouse" above. Marion changed the time of day to sunrise and used rumpled fabric and yarn embellishments.

Land's End
by Barbara S. Bletch,
1995,
Hyattsville,
Maryland,
25½" x 30".
What a great fabric
selection! Barbara
fringed her water
fabric to create the
spray on the rocks.

**Sights of the
Chesapeake:
Skipjack at
Thomas Point**
by Bette Mock,
1995,
Bowie, Maryland,
20½" x 17¾".
Wonderful
embellishments!
Note the couched
chenille yarns
forming the
lighthouse supports.
A button becomes
the boater's head,
and quilting lines
become the waves.
Many appliqué
details, such as
the flag, birds,
and sails, are
three-dimensional.

Monet's "Cliff Walk at Pourville" by Marion R. Wise, 1995, Bowie, Maryland, 21"x 18". Marion's interpretation of Monet's painting includes chopped scraps in the cliff shadows. Marion used yarn for the bushes, wool for the clouds, and she thread-painted the ladies.

Winter Night by Rebecca Plummer, 1995, Bowie, Maryland, 15"x 16". This delicate scene captures the peace of a winter's night. Becky used her own technique of thread painting on tulle for the bare trees and a piece of sequined lace for the tree with Christmas lights. A tulle overlay accents the lavender sky.

Tornado
by Joan Blalock,
1994,
Bowie, Maryland,
43" x 27".
This quilt
commemorates an
approaching tornado
that I watched with
my mom. Luckily, it
veered off before it
reached us.

Autumn Splendor
by Florence E. Marion,
1995,
Bowie, Maryland,
21½" x 18¼".
Along with
"Colorado!"
(page 29),
"Beauty in My
Own Back Yard"
(page 33),
and "Chincoteague!"
(page 34), this piece
completes Flo's Four
Seasons series.
She used heavy
embellishment with
chopped scraps and
machine thread
painting for her
autumn woods.

New Hampshire Delight by Phyllis Zwirko, 1995, Glenn Dale, Maryland, 27⅜" x 26⅜". Phyllis used vertical piecing for the trees and the side of the cliff. Some of the fabrics were airbrushed. Note the use of organza and quilting lines to create the waterfall. Fabric paint and metallic threads enhance the shallow water and foam in the foreground.

At Home in the Woods by Karen Marion, 1995, Nashua, New Hampshire, 30" x 24¾". Karen learned the techniques for making quilted landscapes from her mother, Florence E. Marion, and used them to design a beautiful contemporary piece. Vertical piecing in the house against the horizontal piecing in the tree trunks helps create a sense of the dappled, flickering light in the woods.

Smoky Mountain Fall
by C. Renee Hunt,
1995,
Bowie, Maryland,
20½" x 17".
Renee grew up
in Chattanooga,
Tennessee, so the
Smokies are one
of her favorite
scenes. She created
the fall foliage with
red and yellow
chopped scraps.

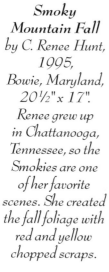

Summer Dawn
by Joan Blalock,
1993,
Bowie, Maryland,
28" x 22".
I used pearlescent
organza to create the
reflections of sunrise.
For a variation of this
piece, see "Sunset II"
on page 48.

Mermaid's Garden
by Joan Blalock,
1991,
Bowie, Maryland,
30½" x 40".
I created this quilt for a guild challenge. The required fish fabric became the star flowers in the garden. Flowers are backed with lamé. Embellishments include couched yarns, a three-dimensional mermaid, painted coral, and a tulle overlay in the water.

Mommy, the Ocean Kissed My Feet
by Kimberly I. Mehalick,
1995,
New Carrollton, Maryland,
18" x 12".
Kimberly's first landscape commemorates a family trip to the ocean. This blue-and-orange color scheme shows a good use of a complementary palette.

Embellishing the Landscape

General Information

This section of the book covers techniques I use to embellish my landscapes. I designed the six small projects in this book to give you an opportunity to play with different embellishment techniques while making a small wall hanging. All of the designs start out with string-pieced backgrounds. (See "String Piecing" on pages 16–18.)

Use the original drawings on pages 82–87 for the small projects so you can concentrate on the embellishment techniques without taking the time to design a pattern. Feel free to change the patterns and/or the embellishments if you come up with better ideas of your own. Refer to "Making the Master Pattern" on pages 13–15 to enlarge the original drawings using a grid system. See "Basic Method" on pages 12–27 to prepare construction patterns, sew the string-pieced sections, add borders, and complete the quilt.

This section includes techniques such as creating details with fabric paint and inks; creating reflections and sparkle with netting, tulles, and organzas; and portraying the roughness of a tree trunk with textured yarns. Other techniques include three-dimensional bushes (using elastic thread) and trees (using fusible web). Additional methods include painting with thread, creating fabric grass clippings, using fabric markers for special effects, and vertical string piecing.

My own work is intuitive, rather than planned. My inclination is to use embellishments as problem solvers; embellishing a section that usually doesn't look as I originally envisioned it (such as after it has been string-pieced). I select the technique that will most easily create the look I have in mind. Sometimes this approach creates more problems than it solves, but I learn a lot with each process, and what I learn can always be used in the next project if it doesn't work for this one.

Supplies for Embellishments

Please refer to the supply list on pages 6–11 for general supplies needed to make your quilt. In addition, you will need a few more supplies to make the projects on the following pages:

■ Assorted cotton print strips in colors appropriate to your design (These can be cut 7/8" to 1 1/4" wide from scraps in various lengths.)

■ 1/8-yd. pieces of several colors of pearlescent organza, fine netting or tulle, and any other special fabrics.

■ Chopped scraps (See "Azaleas" on pages 68–73.)

■ A variety of specialty threads, including metallic thread and rayon or cotton machine-embroidery thread

■ Yarns for couching (I like to combine chenille and bouclé yarns in variegated "tree" colors.)

■ Fabric paints and brushes (For "Cabin in the Pines" only, see page 45.)

■ Fabric markers in dark blue, brown, black, lavender, and dark green

■ Water-soluble glue stick for temporarily holding fabric strips and seam allowances in place.

■ Aleene's™ Hot Stitch glue for fusing tulle and chopped scraps

■ Scraps of fusible webbing (such as Stitch Witchery®—the kind that does *not* have paper backing)

■ Scrap fabrics for practice, including small pieces (12" x 12") of the main fabrics and the batting you will use in your picture

■ 1/2 yd. bleached muslin for painting

■ White plastic lids (the size of 3-pound coffee-can lids), paper cups for water, paper towels, and clear plastic to protect your work surface

■ Teflon pressing sheet to lay over your work when fusing fabric

Note: *Before you begin working on a project, please read through all the instructions. You will not need all the items listed here for every piece.*

Projects

Cabin in the Pines

Finished size:
15¼" x 14¾"

Making this project, you will learn how to paint details and use three-dimensional shapes to embellish the quilt. "Tranquillity" (page 30) has painted details. "Lac Lemon" (page 29) and "Sights of the Chesapeake: Skipjack at Thomas Point" (page 36) make good use of three-dimensional shapes. "New Hampshire Delight" (page 39) uses both embellishment techniques.

Cabin in the Pines by Joan Blalock, 1995, Bowie, Maryland, 15¼"x 14¾".

MATERIALS

44"-wide fabric

In addition to the general supplies listed on pages 6–11 and 43, you will need the following:

Assorted strips of cotton prints in muted lavenders, slate blues, lilacs, and grays for pieced sky and hills, or use 1 fat quarter (9" x 22") of hand-dyed fabric for sky

Assorted scraps of dark green cotton prints for trees

1 square, 6" x 6", of muslin for cabin

¼ yd. blue cotton print for border and binding

1 fat quarter (18" x 22") or ⅝ yd. cotton for backing

18" x 21" rectangle of batting

Fabric paints in orange, slate blue, red, white, green, and navy blue or black

¼"- or ½"-wide inexpensive nylon brush

Lavender fabric marker

Scraps of lightweight fusible web

Teflon pressing sheet

Background Assembly

1. Using the original drawing on page 82, make a master pattern and a construction pattern. Refer to "Making the Master Pattern" on pages 13–15 for enlarging the original using a grid system, and "Making the Construction Pattern" on pages 15–16.

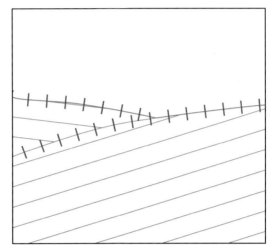

2. String-piece each section. Sew the distant hill (2) to the sky section (1), then attach foreground hill section (3). (See "Assembly" on pages 16–21.)

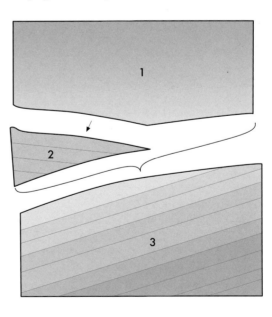

Embellishments

1. Place the square of muslin over the cabin on the master pattern. Trace the cabin's shape onto the muslin.

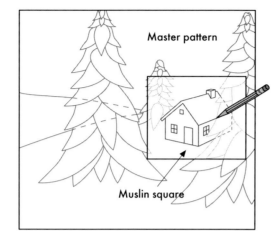

2. Pour a small amount of orange fabric paint onto your plastic palette (one of the lids you've collected). Mixing small amounts at a time, add a bit of black or navy blue to the orange paint until the desired brownish color is reached. Paint the cabin walls.

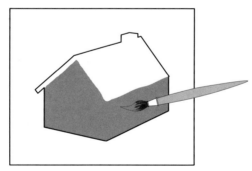

3. When dry, add details with black or blue, such as lines for the boards, door and window frames, and shadows under the eaves. Paint green curtains in the windows if desired. Use the corner of the brush to get very fine lines.

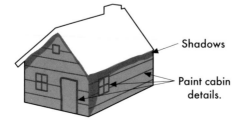

Shadows

Paint cabin details.

4. Paint the roof slate blue, leaving some areas of white to represent snow on the roof, and paint the chimney red, using a darker red for the shadowed side.

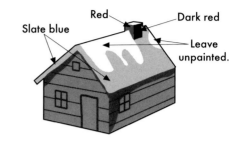

Red — Dark red

Slate blue — Leave unpainted.

5. Using a lavender fabric marker, make light streaks across the white for reflections of the sky on the rooftop snow.

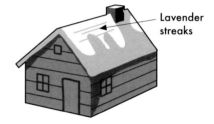

Lavender streaks

6. When dry, cut out the cabin, leaving a ¼"-wide seam allowance. Heat-set the paint. Press the seam allowances under, and using the machine blind stitch or blanket stitch, attach the cabin to the background. Pivot at the corners with the needle down in the background fabric.

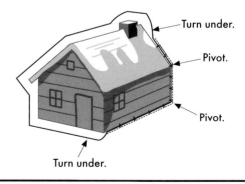

Turn under.

Pivot.

Pivot.

Turn under.

7. Iron the quilt top, then remove the paper pattern.

8. Cut 2 border strips, each 1¾" x 17", for the sides. Cut 2 border strips, each 1¾" x 17½", for the top and bottom. Attach border strips to the quilt. (See "Mitered Borders" on pages 24–25.)

9. For the pine trees, cut enough teardrop shapes from assorted dark green and navy blue scraps to make branches for 3 trees. Cut extras so you have enough to play with. Cut your own teardrop shapes or use the templates provided on page 82, reversing templates as necessary to cut branches for both sides of each tree.

10. Tint white fabric paint with blue-green, lavender, and pink to make 3 colors for the snow on the branches. Paint each teardrop shape with one of the colors, leaving some of the edges (especially the lower ones) unpainted to create the illusion of pine needles peeking out from under the snow. At the tip or along one edge of the shape (an unpainted edge), cut slits at ⅛" (or less) intervals and ¼" to ½" long.

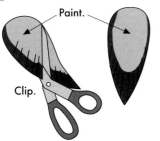

11. Arrange the branches on the picture, placing a small scrap of fusible web under each branch. Work from the bottom of the tree to the top. For the tree on the right, overlap the branches into the border.

12. Place a Teflon pressing sheet over the tree branches and press with the iron to fuse, following the manufacturer's instructions.

13. If desired, add a few machine stitches at the top of each branch to fasten it securely. (I did this step later as part of the quilting.)

ARTIST'S TIP

Use an opalescent thread and stitch along the line where the branch would be under the needles, leaving the sides and lower edges free.

Final Touches

Refer to pages 21–27 to finish your quilt.

1. Trim, if necessary, to square up the piece.

2. Layer the quilt with backing and batting. Pin-baste the quilt.

3. Quilt as desired or follow the quilting suggestion below. Square up the quilt.

4. Bind the edges and add a hanging sleeve. Don't forget to sign and date your work.

ARTIST'S TIP

I quilted details on the cabin with dark brown rayon embroidery thread and used lavender rayon thread for the snow.

Sunset II

Finished size:
15" x 18"

This variation of "Summer Dawn" (page 40) incorporates vertical string piecing and "grass-clipping" embellishments with the basic method. For other examples of vertical piecing, see "At Home in the Woods" (page 39) and "New Hampshire Delight" (page 39). My scene uses intense colors in the sky and water to evoke a tropical sunset, but feel free to change the mood with your own color choices.

Sunset II by Joan Blalock, 1995, Bowie, Maryland, 15"x 18".

Note: *Use the outline of the tree trunks as cutting lines also; put hash marks where the trunks meet the rest of the picture. You will construct this differently from the other projects in the book to accommodate the vertical tree-trunk sections.*

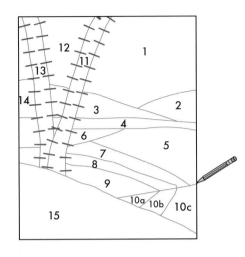

MATERIALS

44"-wide fabric

In addition to the general supplies listed on pages 6–11 and 43, you will need the following:

Assorted strips of cotton prints in blues, lavenders, apricots, yellows, greens, and browns for sky, water, hills, and tree trunks

Assorted scraps of cotton prints in greens, rusts, and browns for grass

¼ yd. brown cotton for border and binding

1 fat quarter (18" x 22") or ⅜ yd. cotton for backing

18" x 22" rectangle of batting

Background Assembly

1. Using the original drawing on page 83, make a master pattern and a construction pattern. Refer to "Making the Master Pattern" on pages 13–15 for enlarging the original using a grid system, and "Making the Construction Pattern" on pages 15–16.

2. String-piece each section except the tree trunks. (See "Assembly" on pages 16–18.)

ARTIST'S TIP

For the sky, use blues, lavenders, apricots, and yellows. For the hills, use greens and browns. For the water, use yellows, apricots, lavenders, and blues. For the tree trunks, use browns.

3. Join Sections 1–7. (See pages 19–21.)

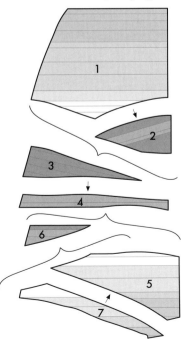

ARTIST'S TIP

Vertical sections are much easier to piece as separate units, rather than string piecing them horizontally within the other sections. By string piecing these sections vertically, you do not need to change strips as frequently within a narrow pattern section, reducing the number of seams (which add bulk) and color changes you must try to match.

4. String-piece the tree trunks. To vertically string-piece, sew the strings along the length of the pattern section so they appear as vertical strips instead of the horizontal strips you sewed in step 2.

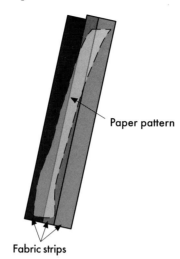

Paper pattern

Fabric strips

5. Make grass clippings to insert between Sections 7 and 8. Use small scraps of green, gray green, brown, and any other appropriate colors of varying lengths that are no narrower than 1" wide. (If you have made other landscape scenes, use leftover strips from them.)

To make each grass-clipping strip, cut slits along one long edge to within ¼" from the opposite edge of the scrap. Cut them about ⅛" apart or as close as you can make them without having the scrap fray or fall apart.

6. Place one or more grass-clipping strips, right side up, on the lower edge of Section 7. Pin or baste in place.

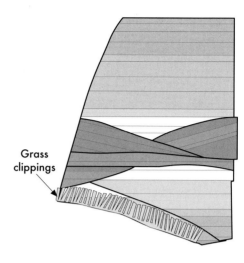

Grass clippings

7. String-piece Section 8. Stitch Section 8 to Section 7, being careful to catch the grass-clipping strip in the seam.

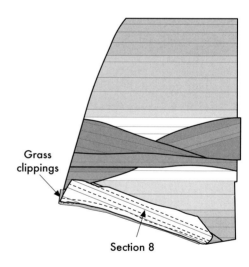

Grass clippings

Section 8

8. String-piece Section 9; sew to Section 8.

9. String-piece Section 10a, b, and c; stitch together, then sew to Section 5/7/8/9.

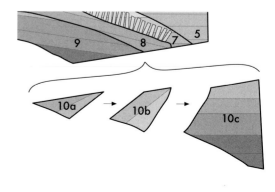

10. Sew tree trunk (Section 11) to the unit made in step 9.

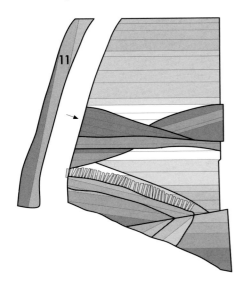

11. String-piece the remaining upper Sections 12–14 of the quilt, using vertical string piecing for the second tree trunk (Section 13). Join the sections.

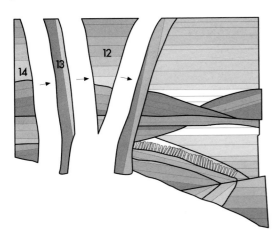

12. String-piece foreground Section 15, following the contour of the land and placing grass-clipping strips between the string-pieced strips as desired.

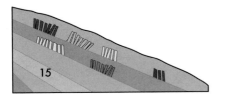

13. Place several clumps of grass-clipping strips at the base of the tree trunks. Layer strips of varying widths, if you like, placing them randomly on the quilt. Pin or baste in place. Sew Section 15 to the quilt. Iron the quilt top, then remove the paper pattern.

Final Touches

Refer to pages 21–27 to finish your quilt.

1. Trim, if necessary, to square up the piece.

2. Cut 2 border strips, each 1¾" x 20", for the sides. Cut 2 border strips, each 1¾" x17", for the top and bottom. Attach border strips to the quilt, mitering the corners.

3. Layer the quilt with backing and batting. Pin-baste the quilt.

4. Quilt as desired or follow the quilting suggestion below. Push the grass aside as you quilt, so it will not be caught in the stitching. Square up the quilt if necessary.

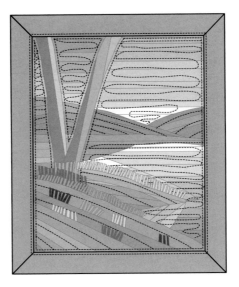

5. Bind the edges; attach a hanging sleeve. Don't forget to sign and date your work.

At the Beach

Finished size: 19½" x 16½"

I planned this scene to be a clear day with blue sky, the ocean varying from blue-green to dark blue-violet. Somewhere between planning and sewing, the quilt took over, wanting to be a morning where the sun is trying to come out after a rain squall. Left-over haze and mist remains from the rain and obscures the horizon. The resulting scene is more abstract than the rest of the projects. When a quilt wants to be something other than what I plan, I usually let it happen, rather than fighting the piece all the way.

In addition to practicing organza and tulle overlaying techniques (to represent ocean waves and wet sand on the beach), you will gain experience with free-motion sewing and thread-painting techniques. See "Colorado!" (page 29) and "Chincoteague!" (page 34) for good thread painting. Refer to "Serenity" (page 30) for an example of fabric overlays.

At the Beach by Joan Blalock, 1995, Bowie, Maryland, 19½" x 16½".

MATERIALS

44"-wide fabric

In addition to the general supplies listed
on pages 6–11 and 43, you will
need the following:

Assorted strips of cotton prints in purples,
    lavenders, grays, golds, yellows, apri-
    cots, and rusts for sky, ocean, waves,
    hill, and beach
⅛ yd. or scraps of purple, lavender, yellow,
    dark gold, and white tulle for waves
Assorted scraps of pearlescent organza for
    ocean
Assorted scraps of lavender and white
    nylon organdy for birds
¼ yd. rust cotton for inner border and
    binding
¼ yd. purple cotton for outer border
1 fat quarter (18" x 22") or ⅝ yd. cotton for
    backing
18" x 21" rectangle of batting
Specialty threads such as opalescent, silver
    stream lamé, and variegated lavender
    metallics; white, light, and medium gray
    rayon threads
Aleene's Hot Stitch glue and/or scraps of
    fusible web
2 scraps, 12" x 12" or larger, of water-soluble
    or heat-dissolving stabilizer
Teflon pressing sheet
7" or 10" machine-embroidery hoop

Background Assembly

1. Using the original drawing on page 84,
make a master pattern and a construction
pattern. Refer to "Making the Master Pattern"
on pages 13–15 for enlarging the original
using a grid system, and "Making the Construction Pattern" on pages 15–16.

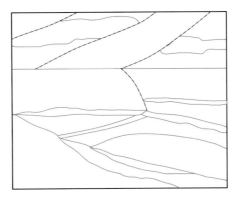

2. String-piece each sky section, then sew
the sections together in the order given. (See
"Assembly" on pages 16–20.)

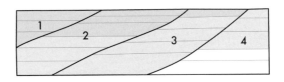

3. String-piece the distant ocean sections.
Lay a piece of pearlescent organza over the
cotton strip for the crest of the large wave in
the right section. Treat the two layers as one
fabric. The organza adds shimmer to the cotton so it resembles water. Join ocean sections.

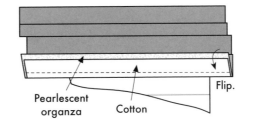

Pearlescent organza   Cotton   Flip.

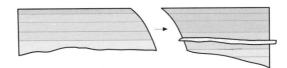

ARTIST'S TIP

*For the sky, use
lavenders, golds,
yellows, and apricots.
For the ocean and
waves, use shades of
purples and golds.
For the beach, use
lavenders, grays,
and yellows. For
the hill, use rusts.*

4. Sew the sky section to the completed ocean section.

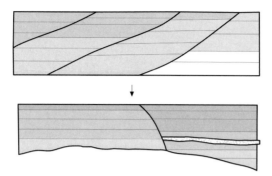

5. Make the crest of the wave on the left by layering a pearlescent organza strip over a cotton strip. With a diagonal seam, sew this combined strip to the right end of a cotton strip, then string-piece the rest of the wave to this pieced strip. Place a scrap of lavender tulle over this section; pin or baste in place. (Later, when you sew the left wave section to the right wave section, treat the two layers as one fabric.)

Cotton strip

Pearlescent organza

Wave crest

Lavender tulle

6. String-piece the large wave on the right. Layer a piece of pearlescent organza over a cotton strip and sew to the left of the wave.

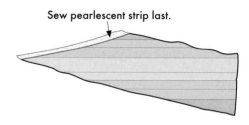

Sew pearlescent strip last.

7. Make the large crest in the wave at right by layering and sewing a 5" x 8" rectangle each of lavender and white tulle across the top of the wave.

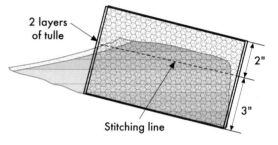

2 layers of tulle

Stitching line

2"

3"

8. Fold the top section of the tulle forward, leaving a ½" tuck; then, following the illustration below, continue folding to make a "bump" that looks a little like foam across the crest of the wave. Pin or baste in place.

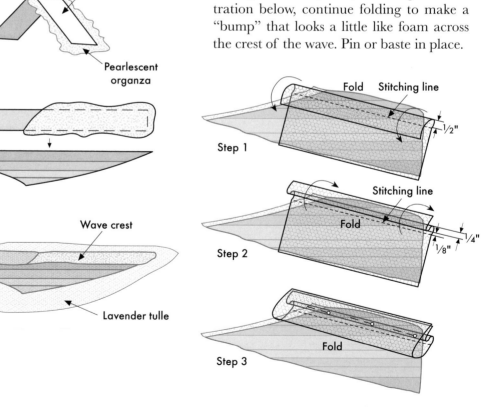

Fold   Stitching line

½"

Step 1

Stitching line

Fold

¼"

⅛"

Step 2

Fold

Step 3

9. Place a white tulle scrap on the wave, beginning just below the curve at the wave's base and extending it over the top of the wave to look like spray. Fold part of the tulle and pleat it randomly in places to create fullness. Pin or baste in place.

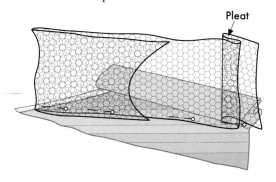

Pleat

10. Fold the left corner of the tulle behind itself and pin in place.

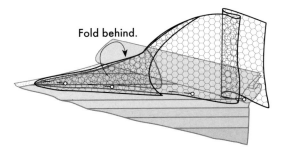

Fold behind.

11. To create the rise of the wave, straight-stitch back and forth from the lower edge of the tulle to the lower edge of the wave's crest, using opalescent metallic thread.

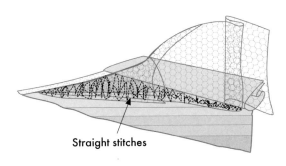

Straight stitches

12. Sew the two wave sections together, then sew to the ocean section. Make sure to keep

the top of the white tulle "spray" free of the stitching.

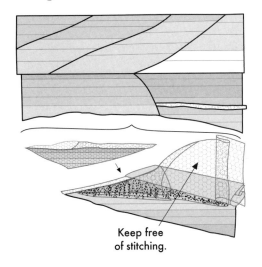

Keep free
of stitching.

Note: *When you sew the wave section to the ocean section, remember to catch the top edges of the lavender tulle bump you made in step 8 into the seam.*

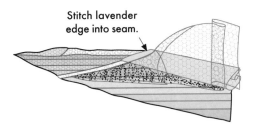

Stitch lavender
edge into seam.

13. String-piece the beach and foreground hill sections, then sew the sections together. Sew this section to the wave section.

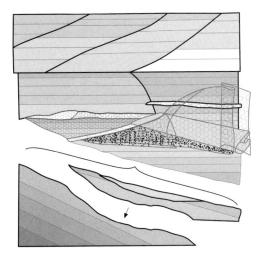

14. Iron the quilt top, then remove the paper pattern.

Embellishments

Layering irregularly cut shapes of organza and tulle on the quilt top creates color variations and shimmer in the ocean.

1. Following the manufacturer's directions, brush a bit of Hot Stitch glue onto the areas of the quilt top where you wish to place the tulle and organza.

2. Cut out the fabric shapes and place them on top of the glued areas, referring to the illustration below or using your own design. Place the Teflon pressing sheet over the fabrics and press, following the manufacturer's directions.

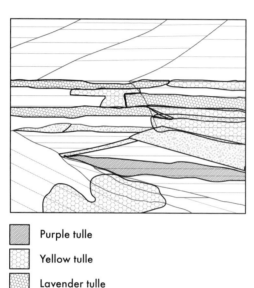

- Purple tulle
- Yellow tulle
- Lavender tulle
- Pearlescent organza

3. To make the large seagulls, sandwich a scrap of water-soluble or heat-dissolving stabilizer between 2 layers of nylon organdy. Trace the bird outlines from the master pattern onto one of the pieces of organdy.

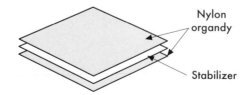

Nylon organdy

Stabilizer

4. Place this "sandwich" in your hoop "inside out," or the opposite way you were taught for hand embroidery. Place the outer ring of the hoop on a table or flat surface.

Set the organdy/stabilizer sandwich face up over the outer ring and center the design. Set the inner ring inside the outer ring and pull the fabric as tight as a drum.

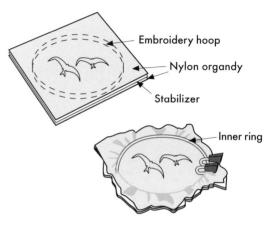

Embroidery hoop

Nylon organdy

Stabilizer

Inner ring

5. Set up your machine for free-motion sewing by either lowering or covering the feed dogs. (See "Quilting" on page 22.) Lower the pressure on the presser foot and adjust the top tension if needed. Thread your machine with light gray rayon thread on top and white all-purpose thread in the bobbin. Make a practice piece first with the thread you will use for the seagulls.

6. Begin stitching along an edge of the design. Holding the end of the top thread, take 1 stitch. Pull the bobbin thread up to the top and hold both threads in place while taking 2 or 3 tiny stitches. Stop in the needle-down position and clip the threads.

7. Hold the hoop with your fingertips, using just enough pressure to guide the hoop. Keep the hoop flat against the machine bed and move it slowly so the needle stitches in the direction the feathers grow. Run the machine as fast as possible without breaking the thread.

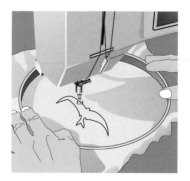

8. Referring to the illustration below, fill in the bird lightly with light gray stitches, then thread the top of the machine with white rayon thread. "Draw" the tops of the feathers and the lightest areas. Switch to medium gray thread to shadow under the wings and define the bird bodies. When you are finished stitching, run 2 or 3 stitches in place and remove from the machine. Clip the thread ends.

Stitch in the direction of the arrows.

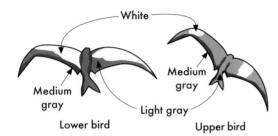

White

Medium gray

Medium gray

Light gray

Lower bird

Upper bird

9. Trim the excess fabric around the birds. Trim as close to the stitching as possible without cutting the threads. Set the completed birds aside to attach after quilting.

Final Touches

Refer to pages 21 – 27 to finish your quilt.

1. Trim, if necessary, to square up the piece.

2. Cut 2 strips, each 1" x 42", for the inner borders. Cut 2 strips, each 2½" x 42", for the outer borders. Sew a 1"-wide strip to a 2½"-wide strip lengthwise and treat as one border strip. Sew the remaining 2 strips together. Attach border strips to the quilt, mitering the corners.

3. Layer the quilt with backing and batting. Pin-baste the quilt.

4. Quilt as desired or follow the quilting suggestion below. Referring to the original drawing for placement, quilt Vs for distant birds, using medium gray thread. Square up the quilt if necessary.

ARTIST'S TIP

Use variegated metallic thread for quilting the water to give the impression of waves in the distance. As you work closer to the foreground, stitch the quilting rows farther apart to make the waves appear closer. Switch to the stream lamé thread to quilt the foreground wave on the right and the puddles in the sand. Quilt the sky, foreground hill, and beach, using either smoke-colored invisible thread or thread to match the background.

5. Attach the seagulls to the quilt, referring to the original drawing for placement. Position the upper bird so it overlaps the border. *Stitch around the body only* with the medium gray rayon thread, leaving the wings free.

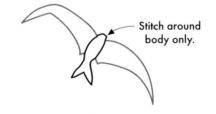

Stitch around body only.

6. Bind the edges; attach a hanging sleeve. Don't forget to sign and date your work.

Fall Tree

Finished size:
14¾" x 17¾"

This scene was taken from a sketch of the area around Woodstock, Maryland, showing a large maple tree wearing its fall colors. By making this quilt, you will gain experience in shading with fabric markers and working with pieced appliqué. I used fabric markers to create the fence and shadows. I also used a marker to visually smooth the edges of the funnel cloud in "Tornado" (page 38). In "Winter Sun" (page 32), I used markers to enhance the orange colors in the sky and make shadows in front of the cabin.

Pieced appliqué makes use of strip piecing to create the look of complex fabric. It is perfect for the foliage of this fall tree.

Fall Tree by Joan Blalock, 1995, Bowie, Maryland, 14¾" x 17¾".

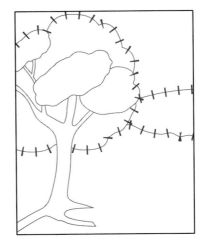

Pattern" on pages 13–15 for enlarging the original using a grid system, and "Making the Construction Pattern" on pages 15–16.

MATERIALS

44"-wide fabric

In addition to the general supplies listed on pages 6–11 and 43, you will need the following:

1 fat eighth (9" x 22") of brown print for tree trunk

Assorted strips of cotton prints in greens, yellow-greens, browns, and light blues for hill, foreground, tree, and sky

15 to 24 cotton strips, in varying widths from 1" to 1½" x 42", of assorted reds, oranges, rusts, and burgundies for tree foliage

¼ yd. burgundy cotton for border and binding

1 fat quarter (18" x 22") or ⅝ yd. cotton for backing

18" x 22" rectangle of batting

Dark blue, dark green, and black fabric markers

Background Assembly

1. Using the original drawing on page 85, make a master pattern and 2 construction patterns (one for the background and one for the tree). Refer to "Making the Master

2. String-piece each section, leaving a 1"-wide seam allowance where the appliqué will overlap the background. (See "Assembly" on pages 16–20.) Sew the distant hill to the sky section, then attach the foreground hill section, creating a hole where the tree will go.

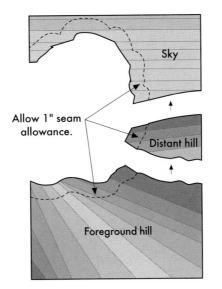

3. Sew 15 to 24 red, orange, rust, and burgundy strips together in random order to make a strip-pieced unit approximately 12½" x 42". (The length of the unit will vary depending upon the length of your strips.) Press seam allowances to one side after adding each new row. Cut across this unit to make strip-pieced segments, randomly varying the widths from 1" to 1½" wide. The number of segments you cut will depend on how wide you cut them.

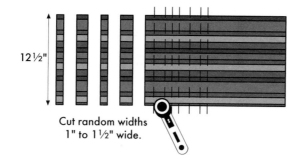

4. Sew the segments together randomly to make a rectangle, approximately 12½" x 17" for the tree-foliage fabric.

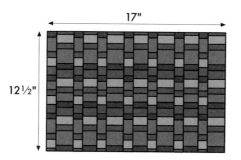

5. Cut out the tree-trunk and tree-foliage patterns from the construction pattern. (For Piece 1, cut 1 large piece to use as a background for appliquéing Pieces 2–5.)

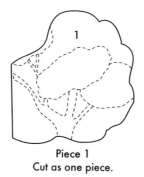

Piece 1
Cut as one piece.

6. Use dabs of glue stick to attach the right side of the tree-trunk pattern to the back of the brown print tree-trunk fabric. Cut out the tree trunk, leaving a ⅛"- to ¼"-wide seam allowance. Press seam allowances under and remove the pattern.

7. Place each foliage pattern on the strip-pieced fabric, turning each piece at a different angle to make a random pattern of

foliage. Cut out the pieces, adding ¼"-wide seam allowances.

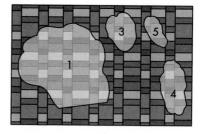

8. For each appliqué piece, press the seam allowance under. (You can hand baste the seam allowance if you prefer or use glue stick.)

9. Carefully place Piece 1 on the background, making sure to overlap seam allowances. Pin or baste in place. Thread the top of the machine with smoke-colored invisible thread, or use a color to match the appliqué piece. Use a neutral gray thread in the bobbin. Machine appliqué, using either a narrow blind stitch or a blanket stitch.

Machine appliqué

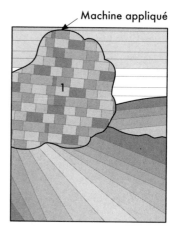

10. Appliqué the tree trunk, then the remaining foliage pieces, in numerical order.

11. Iron the quilt top, then remove the paper pattern. Slit the background behind the tree trunk to remove the paper from the trunk.

Embellishments

1. Using dark blue and dark green fabric markers, fill in the tree's shadow. Refer to page 85 for the shadow's outline. Mark the fabric with the side of the pen's tip, not the point, and use a light touch when applying the ink.

ARTIST'S TIP

Gently stroke the fabric with the side of the marker until the shadow is as dark as you want it. Shadows are usually darker and sharper toward the base of an object, and lighter and less distinct as they move away from the object.

2. Using a black fabric marking pen, draw the fence posts, referring to page 85. Add the wires. (See tip at far right.) The wires and posts become smaller and closer together as they appear to recede from the foreground, helping to establish perspective. Draw the fence-post shadows.

Final Touches

Refer to pages 21 – 27 to finish your quilt.

1. Trim, if necessary, to square up the piece.

2. Cut 2 border strips, each 2" x 22", for the sides. Cut 2 border strips, each 2" x 19", for the top and bottom. Attach border strips to the quilt, mitering the corners.

3. Layer the quilt with backing and batting. Pin-baste the quilt.

4. Quilt as desired or follow the quilting suggestion below. Square up the quilt if necessary.

ARTIST'S TIP

Outline quilting the foliage areas made them puffier than I wanted, so I stipple-quilted the foliage. Because of this extra quilting, the border needed more quilting, so I stitched around the outlines of the printed roses in the fabric.

5. Bind the edges; attach a hanging sleeve. Don't forget to sign and date your work.

ARTIST'S TIP

I used a black fabric marking pen to make the fence posts, and a Pigma pen for the wires. Another method for making the wires is to couch black metallic thread in place. Lay the thread across the quilt, following the master pattern for placement. Extend the ends about 1" beyond the outer edges of the quilt. Using smoke-colored invisible thread and a narrow zigzag stitch, stitch along the wires to couch them in place.

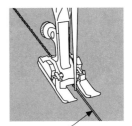

Metallic thread

Early Snow in the High Country

Finished size:

18" x 13"

This scene captures a fall day in the high country, where snow has come early on the tallest mountains. Organza overlays depict snow reflecting the sunlight. Free-motion embroidery creates shadows and pine trees to add to the alpine effect. For examples of organza overlays, see "Lac Lemon" (page 29). See "Beauty in My Own Back Yard" (page 33) for a demonstration of free-motion embroidery. "Early Snow in the High Country" has the most complex piecing sequence in the book.

Early Snow in the High Country by Joan Blalock, 1995, Bowie, Maryland, 18"x 13".

MATERIALS
44"-wide fabric

In addition to the general supplies listed on pages 6–11 and 43, you will need the following:

Assorted strips of cotton prints in greens, blues, pinks, lavenders, browns, navy blues, grays, plums, rusts, yellows, golds, and peaches (light to medium values) for sky, mountains, and hills

⅛ yd. each ice blue and pale pink pearlescent organza for Mountains C, D, and E

⅛ yd. dark gold cotton print for inner border and binding

¼ yd. gold cotton print for outer border

1 fat quarter (18" x 22") or ⅝ yd. cotton for backing

15" x 20" rectangle of batting

Dark brown and dark, medium, and light green machine-embroidery thread for trees

Turquoise and pale gray rayon threads for mountains

Cold-water-soluble stabilizer

7" or 10" machine-embroidery hoop

Background Assembly

1. Using the original drawing on page 86, make a master pattern and construction pattern. Refer to "Making the Master Pattern" on pages 13–15 for enlarging the original

using a grid system, and "Making the Construction Pattern" on pages 15–16.

2. Draw a set of hash marks along the organza stitching lines (or trace the lines on the back of the construction pattern) to help with placement of the organza strips along the edges and top of the mountains.

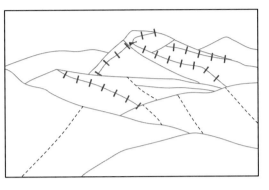

3. String-piece the sky section. (See "Assembly" on pages 16–20.) Since the small area of cloudless sky is not the focus of this scene, piece it as one section.

4. String-piece Mountains A and B. Turn under the seam allowances for the top of Mountain A and lightly glue them to the paper pattern.

5. Set the machine for a blind stitch and, using smoke-colored invisible thread, appliqué Mountain A to the sky section. Set the stitch to the narrowest width. Run the straight stitch along the sky section, next to the mountain, with the "bite" just catching 2 or 3 threads of the mountain.

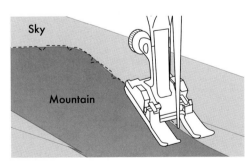

Note: Join the sections right after you piece them to eliminate any chance for confusion. My grandsons were in the sewing room with me as I worked on this piece. With their "help," I discovered that some of the segments look similar if they are accidentally moved.

ARTIST'S TIP

For the sky, use a pale, clear yellow fabric with toned (muted) colors, such as plum, rust, and peach. Choose toned purples, navy blues, and grays, with touches of off-white for snowy areas.

6. Stitch Mountain B to the sky section.

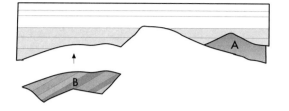

ARTIST'S TIP

Select light to medium lavenders, blues, and pinks for the center mountains, with toned medium plums, blues, and greens for the shadowed areas. At the top of the mountains, where the snow is catching the light, use pearlescent organza: pale pink for Mountain C and ice blue for Mountain D.

7. String-piece Section 1 of Mountain C. Beginning at the left side, lightly glue a strip of light blue or lavender fabric in place, right side up. Cut a 2" x 3¼" strip of organza. Fold it in half lengthwise and place it on top of the first strip, with the fold extending ¼" beyond the seam allowance. Make sure the ends of both strips cover the organza stitching line at the top of the pattern.

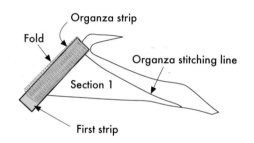

8. Place the second strip of cotton on top of the first 2 strips, right side down and raw edges even. Stitch through all 3 layers. Iron the second strip over the pattern; iron the organza strip over the first strip. Continue piecing the section.

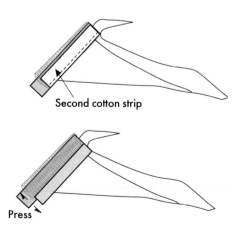

9. Cut a 6" x 7½" rectangle of organza. Fold in half lengthwise. Pin across the top of the section, extending the organza's raw edges ¼" past the organza stitching line. Stitch, then iron the organza strip toward the top of the section. Trim the organza to ¼" from the edge of the paper. Be careful when handling the trimmed organza; it frays easily. Set aside.

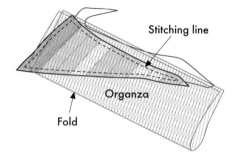

10. String-piece Sections 2 and 3, sewing a strip of organza across the top of Section 3 last. Sew the 2 sections together.

ARTIST'S TIP

Section 2 is a shadowed area. Use darker colors and cut the strips ¾" to ⅞" wide for extra-narrow, finished strips.

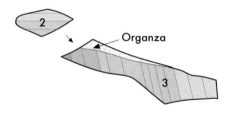

11. Beginning at the right end of the section, pin Section 1 to Section 2/3, pinning only from the outer edge to the point shown below. Be careful to include the organza strip as you sew the two sections together. Stitch between pins, backstitch, and remove from the machine.

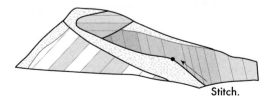

12. Pin from the end of the stitching to the tightest point of the curve. Stitch. Remove from the machine and clip the curves.

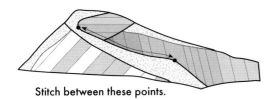

Stitch between these points.

13. Continue pinning and stitching, working on short segments of the seam at a time to make sewing the curved pieces easier.

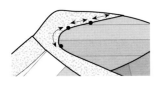

14. Pin Mountain C to the sky section, matching hash marks, then stitch or machine appliqué. (See step 5 on page 63.) If you stitch the mountain to the sky section, pin with right sides together, then sew from the edge to the peak of the mountain. Pin the other side, then stitch from the peak to the edge. If you appliqué the mountain, lightly glue the seam allowance to the back of the paper pattern and appliqué.

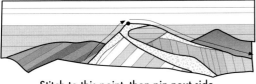

Stitch to this point, then pin next side.

15. String-piece Mountains D and E. When string piecing Mountain D, lay a strip of organza over one or two of the cotton strips, treating them as one layer while you string-piece them. Make sure the ends of the strips overlap the organza stitching line.

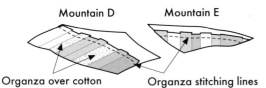

Mountain D | Mountain E

Organza over cotton | Organza stitching lines

16. For each of Mountains D and E, cut a strip of organza to make the snow on the mountaintops. Cut a 3½" x 7¼" rectangle for Mountain D and a 2¼" x 6" rectangle for Mountain E. Referring to step 9, fold the rectangles in half lengthwise and stitch to each mountaintop.

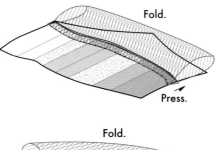

Fold.

Press.

Fold.

Press.

17. Stitch Mountains D and E together, then stitch to the sky/mountain section.

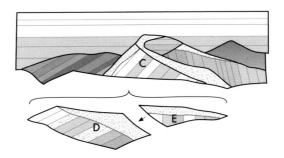

18. String-piece and join sections for Hills A, B, and C. Piece Hills A and B in several sections for a gently climbing, rolling-hill appearance. Note strip orientation arrows on the original drawing.

ARTIST'S TIP

For Hill A, use toned (muted) medium greens. For Hill B, use bright golds to medium browns so the hill looks like it is catching some afternoon sunlight. Use dark to medium browns, with touches of toned greens for Hill C.

Early Snow in the High Country

19. Sew Hill A to the sky/mountain section, then sew Hill C to Hill B. Sew Hills B/C to the quilt.

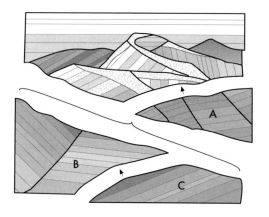

20. Iron the quilt top, then remove the paper pattern. Square up the quilt.

21. Cut 2 strips, each ¾" x 42", for inner borders. Cut 2 strips, each 2" x 42", for outer borders. Sew a ¾"-wide strip to a 2"-wide strip lengthwise and treat as one border strip. Sew the remaining 2 strips together. Measure, trim, and attach border strips to the quilt. (See "Mitered Borders" on pages 24–25.)

Embellishments and Final Touches

There are two methods for free-motion embroidering the trees. Either machine embroider the quilt top before quilting, or stitch through all three layers, so embroidering is part of the quilting process. Practice both techniques and select the one that works best for you.

1. For both methods, trace the tree outlines from the master pattern onto the quilt, using pencil or pen. Make the lines dark enough to see; you will cover them with stitching so they won't show when the quilt is finished.

2. For machine embroidering on the unquilted top, sandwich the tree area between 2 layers of cold-water-soluble stabilizer. Place all 3 layers in the embroidery hoop, making sure it is drum tight.

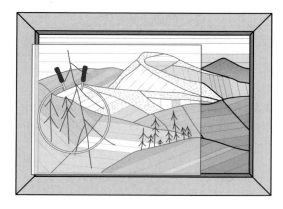

3. Set up your machine and begin "drawing" the trees, following the instructions in steps 5–7 of "Embellishments" for the "At the Beach" quilt on page 56. Use several thread colors (including a light-value green for highlights). Make a practice piece first with the thread you will use for the trees.

4. Begin by drawing the outlines of the trees with medium green, then fill in the trunks, using a zigzag stitch. Change to the dark green and loosely fill in the branches, moving the hoop so the stitching follows the direction that the branches grow. Change to the lighter thread and add highlights sparingly, emphasizing only the areas that catch the light.

Lightest color for highlights

5. After all the branches are stitched, stop with the needle down. Evaluate what you have done so far, checking for areas that need more light or shadow. Go back over these areas if necessary, filling in stitches more heavily.

6. When you have completed the embroidery, remove the stabilizer and press the quilt. Layer with backing and batting. Pin-baste the quilt. (See pages 21– 22.)

7. Quilt as desired or follow the quilting suggestion below. Square up the quilt if necessary. (See page 21.)

8. Bind the edges and attach a hanging sleeve. (See pages 26–27.) Don't forget to sign and date your work.

If you prefer to "draw" and quilt at the same time, be aware that the fabric has a tendency to draw up in areas of heavy free-motion work. For a flat finished piece, quilt evenly and restrict the densely embroidered places to small areas of the quilt.

1. Quilt the entire quilt first, using invisible smoke-colored thread. Be sure to quilt closely or the areas of free-motion will not lie flat. Refer to the quilting suggestion above.

2. Do not use a hoop for this embroidery. Embroider the tree trunks first, then add the branches, referring to steps 3 and 4 on page 66.

3. Add more stitching for highlights and shadows on Mountain C. Work without a hoop, select a free-motion zigzag, and move the fabric from side to side. Stitch the rows closely together, but allow the fabric to show through in places.

Zigzag

ARTIST'S TIP

A zigzag stitch helps to fill in an area more quickly, but the result looks like straight stitches. I chose a gray rayon machine-embroidery thread for the shadow areas. For the highlights, I selected a light turquoise rayon thread.

Light turquoise thread

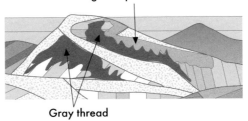

Gray thread

4. Square up the quilt if necessary. (See page 21.)

5. Bind the edges and attach a hanging sleeve. (See pages 26–27.) Don't forget to sign and date your work.

ARTIST'S TIP

All this stitching may cause puckers in the quilt. If this happens, try blocking the piece by ironing with steam and pulling gently on the edges of the piece to flatten it. The borders on my quilt needed extra quilting to lie as flat as the rest of the piece.

Azaleas

Finished size:
15" × 18 ½"

This scene, inspired by a greeting card, includes tiny scraps of cotton specifically chopped to represent the azaleas. Free-motion embroidery and layers of colored tulle scraps create the effect of trees in the distance, highlighted by the sun.

For another quilt that includes the "chopped scraps" technique, see "A View from the Swing" (page 33). For quilts combining both chopped scraps and free-motion embroidery techniques, refer to "Beauty in My Own Back Yard" (page 33) and "Autumn Splendour" (page 38). "Morning Breaks o'er Foxhill Bridge" (page 32) shows effective use of tulle scraps for the trees.

Azaleas by Joan Blalock, 1995, Bowie, Maryland, 15"x 18½".

MATERIALS

44"-wide fabric

In addition to the general supplies listed
on pages 6–11 and 43, you will
need the following:

Assorted strips of blue and green cotton
    prints in light, medium, and dark values
    for sky, water, and foreground
Assorted scraps (no larger than 4" x 4") of
    cotton prints in pinks, burgundies, and
    yellows for azaleas
Small scraps of green, black, navy blue, gold,
    and yellow tulle in light, medium, and
    dark values for trees
2" or 3" of ½"-wide pale green lace for trees
¼ yd. medium blue cotton for border
¼ yd. dark blue cotton for binding
1 fat quarter (18" x 22") or ⅝ yd. cotton for
    backing
18" x 21" rectangle of batting
Dark brown, pink, rose, burgundy, and dark,
    medium, and light green rayon machine-
    embroidery thread
Scraps of fusible web
Dark blue and gray fabric markers
Teflon pressing sheet

Background Assembly

1. Using the original drawing on page 87, make a master pattern and construction pattern. Refer to "Making the Master Pattern" on pages 13–15 for enlarging the original using a grid system, and "Making the Construction Pattern" on pages 15–16.

2. String-piece the sky/land section first, starting with the dark outer strips and working toward the light strips near the horizon line. (See "Assembly" on pages 16–20.)

3. For the narrow strip of land, cut a ¾" x 5¾" strip of pink and a ¾" x 7¼" strip of dark green. (The pink strip represents a distant row of azaleas; the green strip is land). Sew the pink strip to the left end of the green strip, joining them at an angle. To piece the angle, lay both strips, right sides up, on the master pattern and fold the strip of land, following the angle on the pattern. Crease.

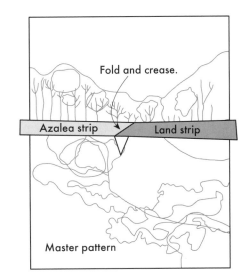

4. Carefully pin the seam allowances of the strips together, keeping the angle accurate. Stitch along the crease. Trim and press seam allowances toward the darker strip. Sew this combination strip to the sky section.

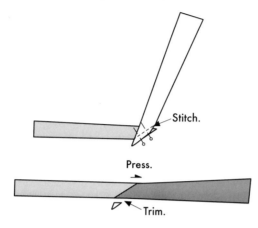

5. String-piece the water section. To show the reflection in the water at right, join strips at an angle to make combination strips as you did for the azalea and land strips in steps 3 and 4. The dark grove of trees that you add later as embellishment causes the reflection, not the land.

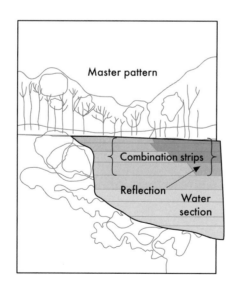

6. Using bright spring greens and yellow-greens, string-piece the foreground hill, following the hill's slope.

7. Sew the foreground hill to the water section, then sew these sections to the sky/land section. Do not remove patterns yet.

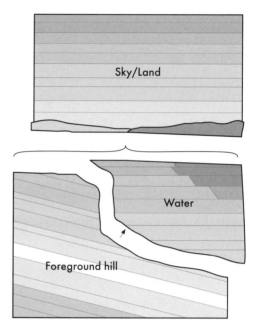

Embellishments

For the trees:

1. Use Hot Stitch glue or fusible web. If you use Hot Stitch glue, sprinkle the glue powder along the general outline of the grove of trees. Using your finger or a brush, spread the powder over the grove area. If using fusible web, place scraps of it over the grove area.

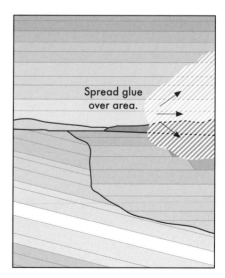

2. Cut scraps (½" to 2" in diameter) of black, navy blue, dark green, and gold tulle for trees. Layer the scraps over the area to define the grove and shadows.

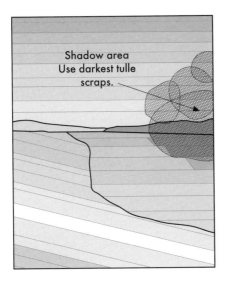

3. Cover the tulle with a Teflon pressing sheet and fuse, following the manufacturer's directions.

4. Place fusible web scraps or sprinkle more Hot Stitch glue over the tulle and across the quilt toward the left side. Cut scraps from the lighter colors of tulle and pale green lace. Scatter them across the quilt for highlights.

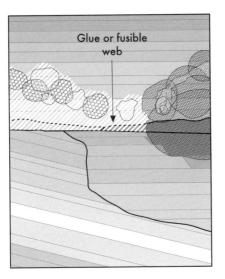

5. Cut a piece of medium green tulle that matches the shape of your grove; place on top of the tulle scraps and fuse.

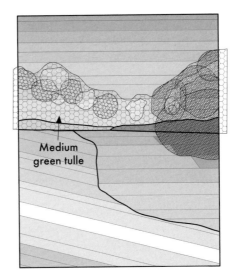

6. Referring to the master pattern for placement, lightly sketch the tree trunks onto the quilt. "Draw" the trunks and branches with one or two lines of free-motion stitching. With the pale green rayon embroidery thread, stitch a free-motion squiggle over the light-colored tulle areas of the trees. Stitch 4 short rows of light green thread to show the highlighted trees reflected in the water. See steps 5 and 6 of "Embellishments" on page 56 for instructions for setting up the machine and free-motion stitching. You do not need a hoop for this stitching.

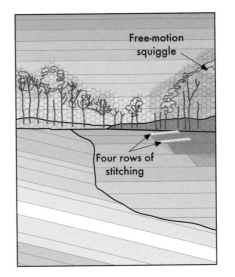

ARTIST'S TIP

Stitch only enough to define the light-colored trees in the foreground and to hold the tulle in place. (Heavy stitching may cause the piece to pucker.) If you catch the tulle in the darning foot, clip the tulle on top of the foot and continue sewing. If necessary, loosen the top tension on the machine to get an even stitch. Practice first to determine the correct setting for your machine.

7. With the dark green rayon thread, embroider free-motion squiggles in the areas of shadow.

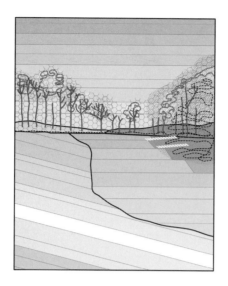

For the azalea bushes:

Chopping the scraps is a process that can help you work out frustration!

1. Working with one fabric at a time, place the scraps for the azaleas on your cutting mat. With a rotary cutter, make random cuts, cutting in one direction, then changing the angle slightly to cut in another direction. Heap the small scraps together and cut again until they are tiny fragments, approximately ¼" x ¼".

ARTIST'S TIP

To keep the colors separate, place each color of fabric scraps in a plastic sandwich bag after cutting.

2. When the chopping is complete, sprinkle glue over the shapes of the bushes on the quilt. Arrange the scraps, defining areas of light and shadow with changes in fabric colors and values.

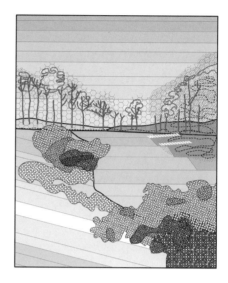

3. Fuse the scraps to the quilt.

4. Stitch a free-motion squiggle over the azaleas, matching rayon embroidery thread to the color of the fabric scraps.

5. Using dark blue and gray fabric markers, create the shadow under the large azalea bush. Stroke lightly with the side of the marker, first blue, then gray, then lightly with blue again.

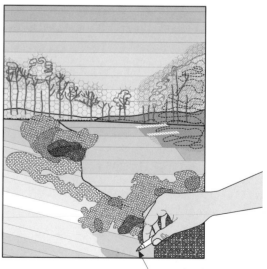

Use side of marker.

6. Iron the quilt top, then remove the paper pattern. (To protect the ironing board, place the Teflon sheet on it first and lay the quilt, right side down, on top. Iron the back of the quilt.) Square up the quilt if necessary. (See page 21.)

Final Touches

Refer to pages 21–27 to finish your quilt.

1. Trim, if necessary, to square up the piece.

2. Cut 2 border strips, each 2" x 19", for the sides. Cut 2 border strips, each 2" x 16", for the top and bottom. Attach border strips to the quilt, mitering the corners.

3. Layer the quilt with backing and batting. Pin-baste the quilt.

4. Quilt as desired or follow the quilting suggestion below. Square up the quilt.

ARTIST'S TIP

*I quilted the azalea bush on the right with a squiggle stitch, using rayon thread to match the flowers and leaves.
I outline-quilted the bushes on the left with invisible thread.*

5. Bind the edges; attach a hanging sleeve. Don't forget to sign and date your work.

Other Embellishments to Try

Gathered Bushes and Shrubs

It is fun to add puffy green bushes to some scenes. "Tranquillity" (page 30) includes this technique.

1. Stretch the fabric for the bush tightly in a hoop. (See the directions for working with embroidery hoops on pages 56–57.)

2. Thread the top of your machine with thread to match the fabric, and use elastic thread in the bobbin.

Note: If your machine won't wind elastic thread on the bobbin, wind the bobbin thread by hand. Some teachers say this method is preferable anyway, since it doesn't stretch the elastic thread.

3. Lower the feed dogs, attach the darning foot, and "draw" small circles in the fabric. The smaller the circles, the tighter the fabric will puff.

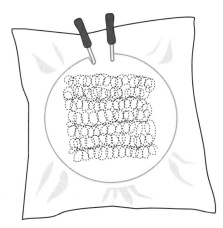

4. Remove the fabric from the hoop and stay-stitch around the shape of the bush.

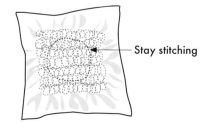

Stay stitching

5. Trim, leaving a ¼"-wide seam allowance, and appliqué in place, turning the fabric edges under at the stay stitching so the stitches don't show.

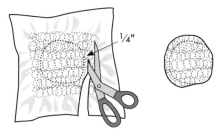

¼"

Microwave Wrinkles

Crinkled fabric is useful for depicting rocky areas, such as the granite sides of a mountain, boulders, and any other rough rocks. I usually use cotton fabrics. Crisp silks, such as shantung and Dupioni, also crinkle nicely. Polyester fabrics do not form crisp lines.

1. Begin with a piece of fabric that is no smaller than a fat quarter (18" x 22"); ½ to 1 yard is better. Accordion-pleat the fabric, in pleats about ½" to 1" wide, to make vertical lines through the crinkles. Making the pleats wider than this looks more like a mistake than a plan.

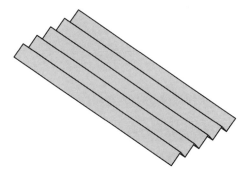

2. Wet the fabric thoroughly and begin to twist from each end. Twist until the fabric starts to double back on itself.

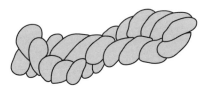

3. At this point, being an impatient type, I do not bother with using rubber bands to secure the fabric, drying it for hours in the dryer, or leaving it alone for days until it is dry (and smells musty). It's faster to double it up and stuff it in a 9- or 14-ounce Styrofoam® cup. (The 14-ounce size will take 1 yard of tightly twisted fabric.)

4. Microwave on high for 2 to 3 minutes. Take it out and let it cool in the cup. If fabric is not thoroughly dry after cooling, microwave for 1 minute more, but *don't* overdo it.

Note: *Watch closely if you add extra time to the microwave. The first time I tried this technique, I added too much time, and the resulting fabric looked burned instead of crinkled. (See below.) If you see steam, take the fabric out of the microwave!*

5. When cool, iron fusible lightweight interfacing to the back of the fabric to hold the wrinkles. Lay the interfacing, sticky side up, on a flat surface. Place the crinkled fabric loosely on the top of the interfacing (right side up). Place a few pins if necessary.

6. Press, fusing the fabric to the interfacing to set the wrinkles.

7. You can also stitch some of the wrinkles to the interfacing to hold them in place. Lift the deeper wrinkles and stitch under them.

8. After securing the wrinkles, cut out shapes as desired.

Couched Trees

This technique is easy and fun to do. My favorite yarns are variegated colors of chenille and bouclé used together. Couching gives a raised and textured look to the branches and tree trunks.

1. Sketch a rough outline of the tree and branches on the background of the quilt or on a piece of organdy if you want to appliqué it later.

2. Pin stabilizer under the fabric. Stitch along the lines with a straight stitch to hold the layers together.

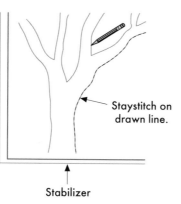

Staystitch on drawn line.

Stabilizer

3. Lay a textured yarn over the staystitched lines. Choose a thread that matches the yarn, or use an invisible monofilament thread. Select a narrow zigzag on the machine and stitch over the yarn.

4. Lay another length of yarn next to the first couched yarn and zigzag in place. Fill in the remaining trunk and branch areas, placing the yarns next to each other and couching to secure them.

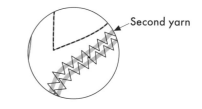

Second yarn

5. Remove excess stabilizer. If you couched your piece on a separate fabric, trim close to the stitching. Thread your machine with smoke-colored thread and appliqué the piece in place, using a narrow zigzag stitch.

ARTIST'S TIP

I try to work the branches first, so the loose ends of yarn will lie under the yarn of the trunk. Whenever possible, try starting the yarn from the edge of the piece, so the border seam will hide loose ends. At the base of the tree, "plant" some grass, using fabric grass clippings, frayed fabric, or more yarns cut in short pieces. In "Sights of the Chesapeake: Skipjack at Thomas Point" (page 36), Bette Mock couched the lighthouse supports, rails, and flagpole using chenille yarn.

Putting It All Together

The embellishment projects on pages 44–73 were designed to cover the seasons, different times of the day, and different areas of the country.

By working through the six projects, you will build a sense of what colors and fabrics best depict a particular time and place and what embellishments to use for the effect you want.

As you walk through your neighborhood or go on vacations, consider carrying a small notebook. Jot down color notes at various times of day and at different seasons. Pick one or two natural objects and note how they appear in the morning, at noon, and at sunset. How are they affected by changing weather conditions or changing seasons? What are the shadows like—clear or fuzzy, long or short? Keeping a "color diary" increases your seeing skills, and the diary can become a terrific resource as you design your own landscapes.

Selecting a Scene

My inspiration comes from a number of sources. Often a magazine or a newspaper photo makes me want to create. Sometimes a piece of fabric talks to me.

"Tornado" (page 38) could also be called "What I Did on My Summer Vacation." I usually spend my vacation in Wisconsin with family. In 1994 I went in July—tornado season. One evening, the sunset changed to darkened skies in an instant. My mother called to me to bring the camera, and the two of us stood, transfixed, watching the storm approach. (Luckily, it changed direction and did not touch down, or the quilt might not have been made.) The snapshots I managed to take captured more of the light and color of the scene than I expected, and the designing was nearly done for me.

Studio art books are good sources for ideas, including coffee-table books and how-to books. Look for these books in art-supply stores and public libraries. If you have access to one or more of these books, you can also use them to study the way other artists have portrayed color and light.

Look through the sources around you: your backyard, vacation photos, books, and magazines. Is there a scene that evokes a strong response or a moment that was especially memorable for you? If so, there's your first "on-your-own" project.

For me, this emotional response is almost physical ("Tornado" is the result of one of these moments). It is as if I can hear the scene or time of day saying "Create me." This emotional energy remains with me as I design the piece. I can hardly wait to get to the piecing, so I can see the picture take form.

Don't wait for it to happen, however. Get started with a scene you like. While working on one scene, inspiration for the next may take shape. Sitting and waiting for inspiration to strike often leads to nothing being done; you need to invite it to happen by continuing to work.

Enlarging a Photo

It's likely the scene you select will need to be enlarged and simplified in order to interpret it in fabric. My own process is to do this by eye, asking myself questions such as:

1. Where is the horizon line in relation to the top and bottom of the scene?

2. What is the size and general shape of the other elements in the picture?

3. Where are these elements in relation to each other and to the horizon line?

4. What is it about this scene that interests me most? Is it the sky, a gnarled old tree, a mountain in the distance, or the reflections on the water?

This last question sets the stage for the picture. The subject I choose will usually be the first object I sketch after the horizon line. Whatever it is, it will be the focal point of the finished piece. Everything else in the scene will be placed so the eye of the viewer is brought back to this point.

For those who would like more structure in this process, I suggest using a sheet of gridded template plastic over your photograph or sketch. Tape the plastic to the picture, so it doesn't slip while you're working.

Count the squares on the template plastic that cover the picture. Draw a grid with the same number of squares, but larger, on your newsprint. If you want a picture that is 12" x 15" and your photo is 3" x 5", I would use template plastic that has four squares to the inch. On the newsprint, draw a grid with 1" squares. Draw your enlargement, one square at a time, repeating the lines in each square of the template plastic in the corresponding square of newsprint. See "Enlarging the Pattern" on pages 14–15.

You may need to omit some details from your plan. Too much in a picture clutters it. Draw only those details that are important to and enhance your focal point. Most of the details in a photo are just background clutter; they do not help the picture and they can seriously complicate the piecing.

High-tech types may find this procedure too tedious. If your image is on a slide, use a projector to project your scene onto a piece of newsprint taped to the wall. If your image is not transparent, use an opaque projector or make a transparency that can be projected on an overhead projector. (Most photocopy shops can do this for you.) If you don't have a projector, try borrowing one from your quilt guild or local library.

When you draw the image onto the newsprint, draw only the lines you want in your scene. Once the enlargement is complete, draw cutting lines (see pages 13–14), then follow the steps on pages 15–27; you're ready to sew your own original design.

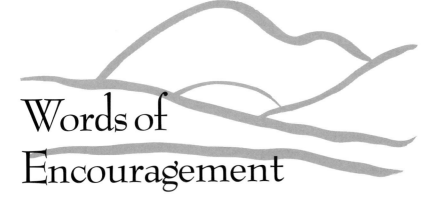

Words of Encouragement

I'm sure that as you work, many of you will go beyond the ideas I provide in this book, just as my students' work in the gallery did. I'd love to see your work in future exhibitions (or in photographs too). It's exciting for me to see where others take these methods.

My landscapes are expanding to include watercolor techniques with more thread painting and embellishment. Who knows where that will lead. May these techniques bring you pleasure and make your landscaping easier; that's the reason for this book.

Suggested Reading

Wolfrom, Joen. *Landscapes and Illusions.* Lafayette, Calif.: C & T Publishing, 1990. See pages 2–9.

James, Michael. *The Second Quiltmakers' Handbook.* Mountainview, Calif.: Leone Publications, 1993. See pages 34–53 for an excellent discussion of color.

Amsden, Dierdre. *Colourwash Quilts.* Bothell, Wash.: That Patchwork Place, 1994. See pages 49–54.

How-to painting books are also helpful resources. Look at how artists in other media handle effects such as haze, light and shade, or the seasons. The following listings have particularly good discussions and color photos:

Willis, Lucy. Light: *How to See It, How to Paint It.* London: Quarto Publishing, 1988.

Poskas, Peter, and J. J. Smith. *The Illuminated Landscape.* New York: Watson-Guptill Publications, 1987.

Supply Sources

For paints and painting tools, write or call the following companies:

Dharma Trading Company
Box 150916
San Rafael, CA 94915
(800) 542-5227
This company responds quickly to phone orders.

Ivy Imports
6806 Trexler Road
Lanham, MD 20706
(301) 474-7347
Fax: (301) 441-2395

Skydye Fabrics
83 Richmond Lane
West Hartford, CT 06117

About the Author

Leland J. Bryant

Joan Blalock received her bachelor's degree in Art Studio after her four sons were in school and while working full-time. Her start in quilted landscapes came after attending a show at Belair Mansion, a local historical site that inspired her to capture its likeness in fabric.

Like most women, Joan is a "juggler." She shares her time with her husband, home, full-time job (at the county jail), and two young grandsons who live with her. In addition, she quilts and teaches quilt classes for shops and guilds. She always has several works in progress and more ideas to try. The more involved she is in quilting, the more she knows that the house will be there whenever she gets to it—quilting is so much more important!

Sunset

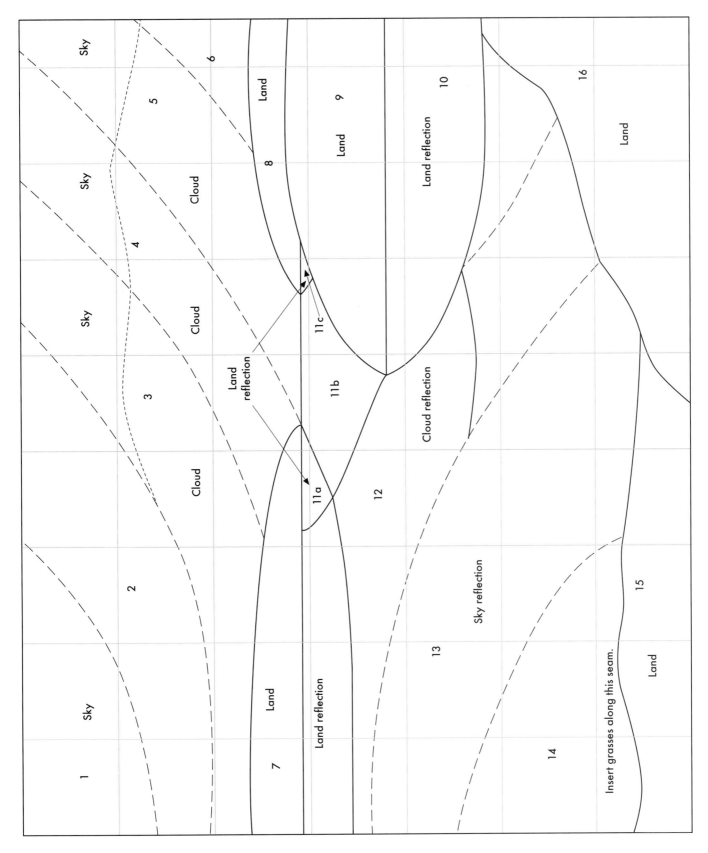

Cabin in the Pines

Branch Templates

Sunset II

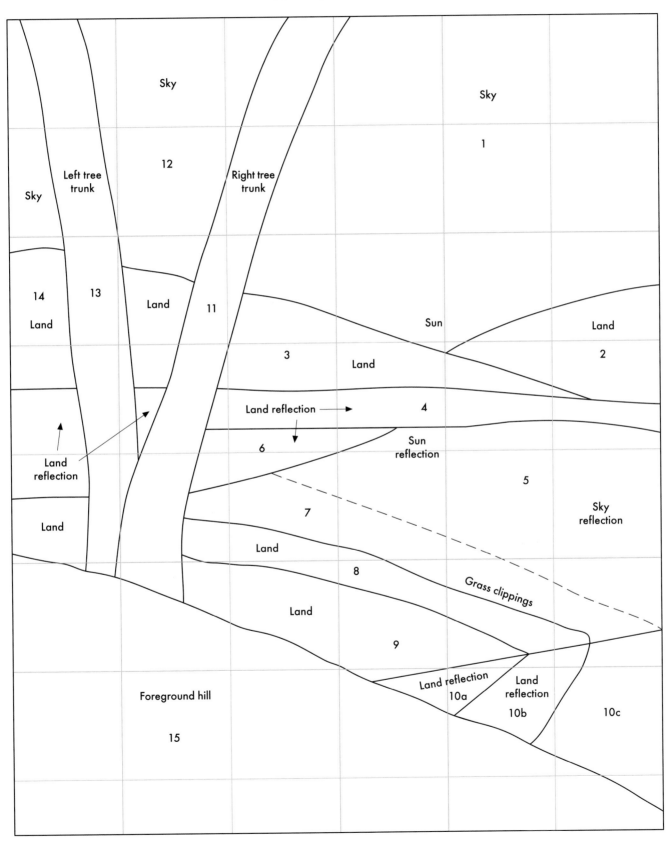

At the Beach

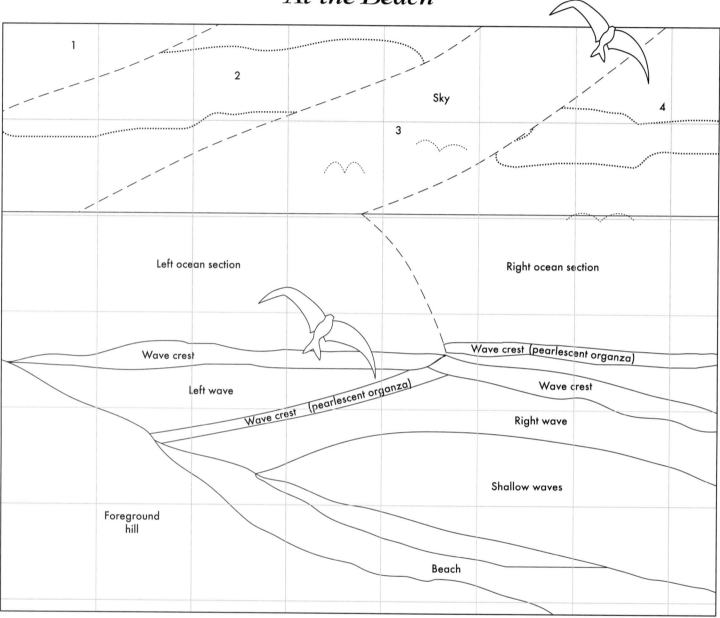

1

2

Sky

3

4

Left ocean section

Right ocean section

Wave crest

Wave crest (pearlescent organza)

Left wave

Wave crest

Wave crest (pearlescent organza)

Right wave

Shallow waves

Foreground
hill

Beach

Fall Tree

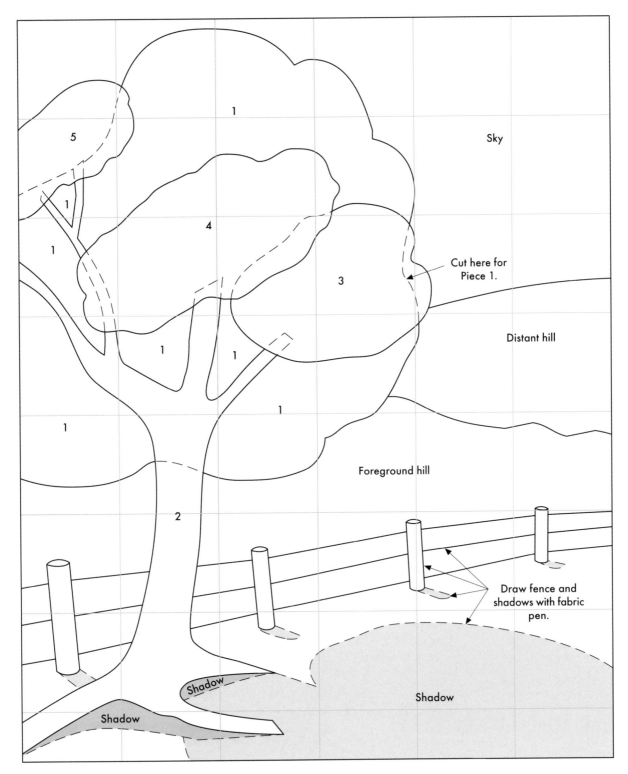

Early Snow in the High Country

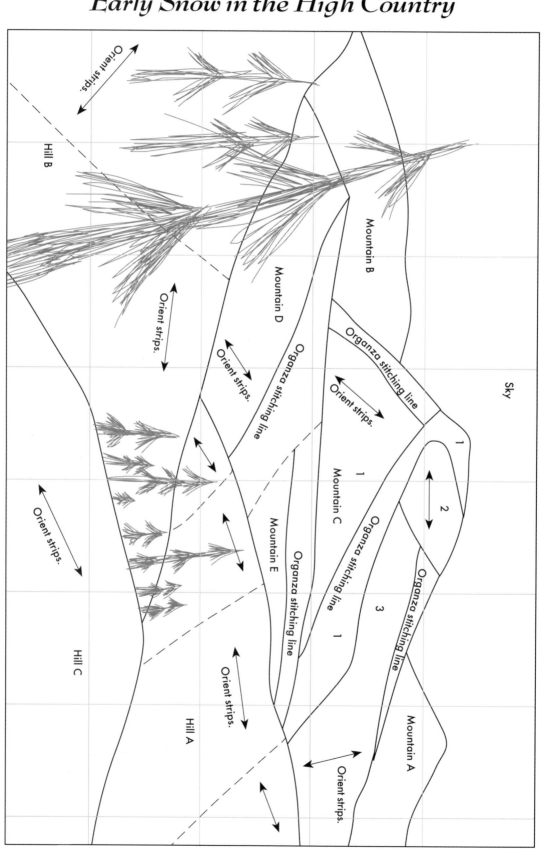

Azaleas

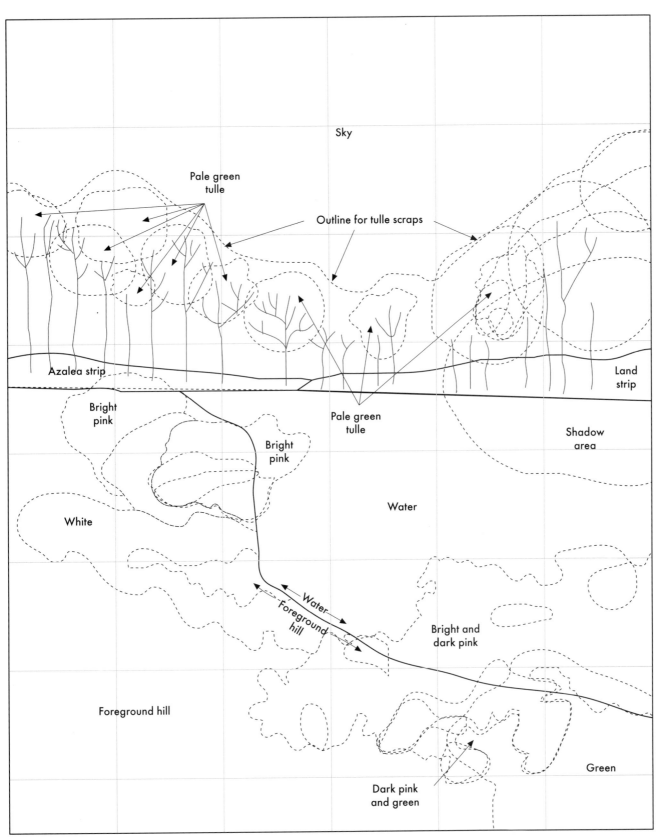

Sky

Pale green
tulle

Outline for tulle scraps

Azalea strip

Land
strip

Bright
pink

Bright
pink

Pale green
tulle

Shadow
area

White

Water

Water

Foreground
hill

Bright and
dark pink

Foreground hill

Dark pink
and green

Green

Publications and Products

THAT PATCHWORK PLACE TITLES:

All New Copy Art for Quilters
All-Star Sampler • Roxanne Carter
Appliquilt® for Christmas • Tonee White
Appliquilt® to Go • Tonee White
Appliquilt® Your ABCs • Tonee White
Around the Block with Judy Hopkins
At Home with Quilts • Nancy J. Martin
Baltimore Bouquets • Mimi Dietrich
Bargello Quilts • Marge Edie
Beyond Charm Quilts
   • Catherine L. McIntee & Tammy L. Porath
Bias Square® Miniatures • Christine Carlson
Blockbender Quilts • Margaret J. Miller
Block by Block • Beth Donaldson
Borders by Design • Paulette Peters
The Border Workbook • Janet Kime
Calicoes & Quilts Unlimited
   • Judy Betts Morrison
The Cat's Meow • Janet Kime
Celebrate! with Little Quilts • Alice Berg,
   Mary Ellen Von Holt & Sylvia Johnson
Celebrating the Quilt
Class-Act Quilts
*Classic Quilts with Precise Foundation
   Piecing* • Tricia Lund & Judy Pollard
Color: The Quilter's Guide • Christine Barnes
Colourwash Quilts • Deirdre Amsden
Crazy but Pieceable • Hollie A. Milne
Crazy Rags • Deborah Brunner
Decorate with Quilts & Collections
   • Nancy J. Martin
Design Your Own Quilts • Judy Hopkins
Down the Rotary Road with Judy Hopkins
Dress Daze • Judy Murrah
Dressed by the Best
The Easy Art of Appliqué
   • Mimi Dietrich & Roxi Eppler
Easy Machine Paper Piecing • Carol Doak
*Easy Mix & Match Machine Paper
   Piecing* • Carol Doak
Easy Paper-Pieced Keepsake Quilts
   • Carol Doak
Easy Reversible Vests • Carol Doak
Easy Seasonal Wall Quilts • Deborah J.
   Moffett-Hall
Easy Star Sampler • Roxanne Carter
A Fine Finish • Cody Mazuran
*Five- and Seven-Patch Blocks & Quilts for
   the ScrapSaver* • Judy Hopkins
*Four-Patch Blocks & Quilts for the
   ScrapSaver* • Judy Hopkins
Freedom in Design • Mia Rozmyn
From a Quilter's Garden • Gabrielle Swain
Go Wild with Quilts • Margaret Rolfe
Go Wild with Quilts—Again! • Margaret Rolfe
Great Expectations • Karey Bresenhan
   with Alice Kish & Gay E. McFarland
Hand-Dyed Fabric Made Easy
   • Adriene Buffington
Happy Endings • Mimi Dietrich
Honoring the Seasons • Takako Onoyama
Jacket Jazz • Judy Murrah

Jacket Jazz Encore • Judy Murrah
The Joy of Quilting
   • Joan Hanson & Mary Hickey
Kids Can Quilt • Barbara J. Eikmeier
Life in the Country with Country Threads
   • Mary Tendall & Connie Tesene
Little Quilts • Alice Berg, Mary Ellen Von Holt &
   Sylvia Johnson
Lively Little Logs • Donna McConnell
Living with Little Quilts • Alice Berg,
   Mary Ellen Von Holt & Sylvia Johnson
The Log Cabin Design Workbook
   • Christal Carter
Lora & Company • Lora Rocke
Loving Stitches • Jeana Kimball
*Machine Needlelace and Other
   Embellishment Techniques* • Judy Simmons
Machine Quilting Made Easy • Maurine Noble
*Magic Base Blocks for Unlimited Quilt
   Designs* • Patty Barney & Cooky Schock
Miniature Baltimore Album Quilts
   • Jenifer Buechel
Mirror Manipulations • Gail Valentine
More Jazz from Judy Murrah
More Quilts for Baby • Ursula Reikes
More Strip-Pieced Watercolor Magic
   • Deanna Spingola
*Nine-Patch Blocks & Quilts for the
   ScrapSaver* • Judy Hopkins
No Big Deal • Deborah L. White
Once upon a Quilt
   • Bonnie Kaster & Virginia Athey
Patchwork Pantry
   • Suzette Halferty & Carol C. Porter
A Perfect Match (revised) • Donna Lynn
   Thomas
A Pioneer Doll and Her Quilts • Mary Hickey
Press for Success • Myrna Giesbrecht
Quilted for Christmas, Book II
Quilted for Christmas, Book III
Quilted for Christmas, Book IV
Quilted Landscapes • Joan Blalock
Quilted Legends of the West
   • Judy Zehner & Kim Mosher
Quilted Sea Tapestries • Ginny Eckley
A Quilter's Ark • Margaret Rolfe
Quilting Design Sourcebook • Dorothy Osler
Quilting Makes the Quilt • Lee Cleland
Quilting Up a Storm • Lydia Quigley
Quilts: An American Legacy • Mimi Dietrich
Quilts for Baby • Ursula Reikes
Quilts for Red-Letter Days • Janet Kime
Quilts from Nature • Joan Colvin
Quilts Say It Best • Eileen Westfall
Refrigerator Art Quilts • Jennifer Paulson
Rotary Riot • Judy Hopkins & Nancy J. Martin
Rotary Roundup
   • Judy Hopkins & Nancy J. Martin
Round Robin Quilts
   • Pat Magaret & Donna Slusser
Sensational Settings • Joan Hanson
Sew a Work of Art Inside and Out
   • Charlotte Bird
*Shortcuts: A Concise Guide to Rotary
   Cutting* • Donna Lynn Thomas
Show Me How to Paper-Piece • Carol Doak
Simply Scrappy Quilts • Nancy J. Martin

Small Talk • Donna Lynn Thomas
Square Dance • Martha Thompson
Start with Squares • Martha Thompson
Strip-Pieced Watercolor Magic
   • Deanna Spingola
Stripples • Donna Lynn Thomas
Stripples Strikes Again! • Donna Lynn Thomas
Strips That Sizzle • Margaret J. Miller
Sunbonnet Sue All Through the Year
   • Sue Linker
Template-Free® Quilts and Borders
   • Trudie Hughes
Threadplay with Libby Lehman • Libby Lehman
Through the Window & Beyond
   • Lynne Edwards
The Total Bedroom • Donna Babylon
Traditional Quilts with Painless Borders
   • Sally Schneider & Barbara J. Eikmeier
Transitions • Andrea Balosky
Tropical Punch • Marilyn Dorwart
True Style • Peggy True
Variations in Chenille • Nannette Holmberg
Victorian Elegance • Lezette Thomason
Watercolor Impressions
   • Pat Magaret & Donna Slusser
Watercolor Quilts
   • Pat Magaret & Donna Slusser
Weave It! Quilt It! Wear It!
   • Mary Anne Caplinger
Welcome to the North Pole
   • Piece O' Cake Designs
Whimsies & Whynots • Mary Lou Weidman
WOW! Wool-on-Wool Folk Art Quilts
   • Janet Carija Brandt
Your First Quilt Book (or it should be!)
   • Carol Doak

4", 6", 8" & metric Bias Square® • BiRangle™
Ruby Beholder® • ScrapMaster • Bias Stripper™
Shortcuts to America's Best-Loved Quilts (video)

FIBER STUDIO PRESS TITLES:
Complex Cloth • Jane Dunnewold
Dyes & Paints • Elin Noble
*Erika Carter: Personal Imagery
   in Art Quilts* • Erika Carter
*Fine Art Quilts: Work by Artists
   of the Contemporary QuiltArt
   Association*
Inspiration Odyssey • Diana Swim Wessel
The Nature of Design • Joan Colvin
Thread Magic • Ellen Anne Eddy
*Velda Newman: A Painter's Approach
   to Quilt Design* • Velda Newman with
   Christine Barnes

Many titles are available at your local quilt shop.
For more information, write for a free color catalog
to Martingale & Company, PO Box 118, Bothell,
WA 98041-0118 USA.

☎ U.S. and Canada, call **1-800-426-3126** for the
name and location of the quilt shop nearest you.
Int'l: 1-425-483-3313   **Fax:** 1-425-486-7596
E-mail: info@patchwork.com
Web: www.patchwork.com   1.98